Manston's Antique Fairs and Auctions of France

[handwritten inscription]

*... and
... a Happy Birthday*

*With love
Ruth xxx*

Manston's Antique Fairs and Auctions of France

Including
where to find markets,
how to ship items,
clear customs,
and much more

by
Peter B. Manston

A Travel Key Guide
Published by B.T. Batsford Ltd.
London

Published in the U.K. by
B.T. Batsford Ltd.
4 Fitzhardinge Street
London W1H 0AH
Telephone 01-486 8484

Published in a different edition
in the United States by
Travel Keys
P.O. Box 160691
Sacramento, California 95816 U.S.A.
Telephone (916) 452-5200

Designed by Peter B. Manston
Cover photo by Robert C. Bynum
Edited in the United States by Robert C. Bynum
    and in the United Kingdom by Alison Bolus
Illustrated by Claudia R. Graham
Type galleys by Lithographics, Sacramento,
    California, U.S.A.
Printed and bound by Interpress Budapest
Manufactured in Hungary
First Printing January 1989

ISBN 0-7134-6235-3

Contents

Acknowledgements

Many people helped provide information and support while this book was being written. Most of them provided help, but it isn't possible to thank them all. A few I'd like to thank specially include: Robert C. Bynum, who aided in field research and provided excellent editorial comments and moral support, Paula R. Mazuski for help in clarifying the objective of this book, Alison Bolus, for her patience in helping adapt the book for the British edition, and Agnes A. Manston (my mother). In addition, we appreciate the help of Bernadette Meauzé for help with correctly writing the French language.

Disclaimer of Responsibility

Markets may move as the result of urban renewal, close during bad weather, or be rescheduled around holidays. Bus lines may be renumbered, car parks may be replaced by buildings, parking garages may raise their rates, and new underground stations may be built.

This book is as complete and accurate as possible. Information has been exhaustively checked and rechecked. Therefore, though the information is deemed to be accurate as of press date, some of it may not exactly mirror your experience; we hope the differences are few and inconsequential. Neither the author nor the publisher can be responsible if you are inconvenienced by information contained in this book.

The persons, companies, institutions, and organizations named in this book are believed to be reputable and engaged in the work they purport to be in. Any questions should be directed to them rather than the publisher or author. Inclusion or exclusion of a firm or organization is no reflection on the suitability of their service or product.

When you find differences, will you let us know? Fill out the "Will You Help?" form at the end of the book or send a letter. What **you** find and suggest can make the next edition even more complete and more useful to those who follow your path.

Introduction

You will find antique markets, antique fairs, auction houses, and flea markets just about everywhere in France—they burst forth in some of the most unlikely places like crocuses blooming through spring snow. Like crocuses, they are tough in spite of their apparent fragility—many have been held at the same location for decades and some for centuries.

At flea markets, antique hand-blown crystal decanters sit next to dusty bronze statues, paintings of indefinite age, all supported by old furniture, rickety tables, permanent stands, or, sometimes, only by the timeworn cobblestones of the street. The babble and hubbub of hundreds of voices makes the scene exciting, full of local color. You can find anything and everything at these flea markets—sinks, scrap metal, old clothes, and cabbages. Though a lot is just plain junk, there are a few lurking treasures.

A French flea market is not the same as a British flea market. A French market is not a place with cheap clothes and new household articles. Rather, it is a market with all kinds of used and antique items—though there may be some new items lurking around.

At hundreds of antique shows and fairs, thousands of dealers display long rows of exquisitely-nurtured antiques of all types and ages: Louis XV furniture, gold 19th-century mantel clocks, and fine, massive silver.

Every region of France has public auctions: the type of items sold under the auctioneer's hammer is unlimited in its variety, from paintings, tapestries, and carpets to old farm implements and country furniture.

In this book, you'll find information vital to the antique dealer and collector:

- when and where to find antique markets, auctions, and shows
- basic antique-market French
- how to ship your purchases home safely
- export requirements for taking fine arts and antiques out of France
- British Customs requirements for taking items home
- and much, much more.

7

To make this book easy to use, a complete index will help you find what you need fast.

This book is dedicated to you, the ever-hopeful collector of exciting experiences and warm memories.

Can You Still Make Finds?

All of us have heard about long-lost masterpieces found in a junk shop or bought for a few pounds at an antique market. We would all like to make a "great find"—a long-lost Watteau, perhaps, or an original Toulouse-Lautrec poster, a piece of original Louis XV furniture, or a solid silver chocolate pot.

These items do exist, and can occasionally be found, usually accompanied by great publicity and newspaper headlines. Finds of this type are rare.

But minor finds can more readily be made—the antique solid silver serving spoon for much less than the cost of silver plate, the finely-detailed century-old newel post wood carving, a minor 17th- or 18th-century artist's painting.

The more you know about a given period or class of objects, the likelier you are to recognize and make a true find. This merely reinforces the fact that specialized knowledge has potentially great value.

Remember, you're searching for the proverbial needle in a haystack; there are thousands of French dealers and collectors in competition for the same things you are.

Since many European dealers only know about specialties of their own locality or country, you can take the broader view, surveying the products of the entire continent. Often, your best finds will be products or artwork far from their home, and whose true value is therefore unappreciated or unknown locally.

Why Search for Antiques in France?

The great artistry of French craftsmen has been renowned for centuries, even before the 17th-century golden age of Louis XIV, the "Sun King", and its dedication to absolute luxury. You find proof in soaring Gothic cathedrals, exquisite detail of Gobelins tapestries, and fine woodwork ranging from inlaid marquetry secretaires to massive country armoires.

France's rich heritage of careful and almost faultless craftsmanship remains active. Today, the best French work for the luxury market is famous for its style and quality.

Only Germany and Britain have as many different markets as France. But no country exceeds France in the variety and quality of items to be found. Though in the years just after World War II antiques and collectables could be found for a trifle, most French today are aware of the value of the things they want to sell. In many cases, though, French prices are far lower than those found in the United States or Canada, and often less than Germany or Switzerland for equivalent work. Of course, the relative strength of dollars, marks, and Belgian and Swiss francs against the French franc could change this. This doesn't mean that things are dirt cheap—only less expensive. What will not change is that France has a much greater wealth of antiques and collectables than you'll find in many other countries.

The world's prototype flea market is the Paris' marché aux puces at the Porte de Saint-Ouen and the Porte de Clignancourt. There is probably no larger market or larger single concentration of antiques, collectables, and junk in the world. Situated just outside the site of ancient but long-demolished city walls, the market arose when the city of Paris forbade throwing rubbish into the streets. Instead, it had to be thrown into containers. Then the rubbish was all carted to this tumbledown habitat of refuse haulers and scavengers. The rubbish was picked over, and anything salvageable was offered for sale: used clothes, broken furniture, discarded silver, and broken crystal.

Though still grimy and weatherbeaten, this area no longer resembles a rubbish dump. Neither do most of the flea markets elsewhere in Paris and the rest of France.

Most French markets and fairs are regional in scope: while Paris draws on the rich heritage of all of France, traditionally rich regions (such as Burgundy and Normandy), and cities (such as Lyon and Bordeaux) have much of local origin to offer. The untouristed, economically declining industrial area around Lille, almost on the Belgian border, also has much to offer the collector and dealer.

Regions in the relatively poor mountain ranges of central France have far less to offer, though finds of folk art (both new and old) can be made by the careful buyer. It's just that there's much less to choose from, though the scenery and rustic charm of these regions alone can justify a visit.

French markets in all but the largest cities are often mixed: antiques and junk form but a small part of the larger market, full of everyday products such as new clothes, kitchen gadgets, cheap plastic items, and, above all, food. While often the antique and junk sellers congregate in a particular part of the market or occupy only one street or small square, sometimes the various kinds of sellers are happily intermingled:

an old peasant may sell carrots, potatoes, and delicate heads of round lettuce next to a whole family selling kitchen items and small, plastic, car-size carpet sweepers, while a young, intense man sells old bottles, tarnished silver plate, and a beautiful late 19th-century cut glass crystal wine carafe.

Search for antiques in France because the variety is endless, the quality of the items is high, and because it's challenging and fun.

Learning to Know
What You See

In France, you'll find antiques, collectables, and assorted items by the thousands. You're limited only by your money, your patience, and your transportation. Good luck and intuition may help you discover an item of real artistic quality, but for the real finds, you must know what you're looking at.

You'll be well repaid later by the effort spent now, when you will know enough to tell a good piece from a poor or fake one while on your own at a boisterous flea market, auction, or antique show. You'll be faced with hundreds and thousands of items, but only a few will interest you, and even fewer will be a very good value for the serious collector.

At well-known dealers and dealers' marts, such as the Louvre des Antiquaires in Paris or Brocante Stalingrad in Lyon, you will often be able to obtain certificates of authenticity and provenance papers, in which the vendor states that you're really buying an antique. Naturally such guarantees and paperwork have their (high) price.

At flea markets and junk shops, however, the motto is "let the buyer beware". The market in fakes sold to the unwary is large, and buyers' cupidity and ignorance are prime sales tools for these sellers.

The time to start learning is right now. Read everything you can—style guides, price guides, antique-trade and fine arts magazines, museum catalogues, and applied arts and fine arts history. Catalogues from Christie's and Sotheby's auctions are treasure-troves of knowledge, with illustrations of sale items, descriptions of the creators, the items, and characteristics of the styles, and estimated sales prices. These catalogues are sometimes available at libraries and museums and, of course, are sold through the auction houses.

Study the text and illustrations carefully— what you remember will make it much easier to sort through the thousands of worthless pieces for the few excellent items later.

Your local library is an excellent place to begin. Look through the "Books In Print" to supplement your search of library shelves—many small and medium-sized libraries can often obtain books through an "interlibrary loan" system. For details and to make a request, see the reference librarian.

College and university libraries have more complete and specialized collections. Usually the public is admitted to "open-stack" libraries and can read the books in the library at no charge. Often you can become a "friend of the library" at modest cost to obtain borrowing privileges.

Museums are another place to learn. In major museums you will be able to see actual examples of authentic, good-quality works. Study the lines, the artistic qualities, and materials carefully. When you have a bit of knowledge but want more, seek out the curators in the museum. If you're particularly interested, curators and staff members can and often will make materials and items available to you. Remember that many museums have much of their collection in storage—there's rarely enough space to display everything. Show at least rudimentary knowledge and scholarly intent to obtain the maximum amount of help and access. Sometimes museums also have excellent art libraries.

Antique dealers in your area represent a valuable source of knowledge. Experts love to share their knowledge with an appreciative audience.

Let your sense of beauty and value for money guide you: learn to trust your instincts, based on a foundation of knowledge.

Origins of the Market

Centuries ago, as the people living in the Middle Ages prospered, European cities began to grow, stimulated by trade in the cloth, foods, and other products of other parts of Europe, and the luxuries of the east.

Great markets and fairs were held in the centres that developed at trade route crossroads, such as Bruges, Ghent, Frankfurt, Lyon, Paris, and Milan. From these, the idea of regular scheduled markets specializing in certain products arose. In a world of slow and uncertain transport (ships reliant on sails, loaded carts drawn by animals, or packs carried by human porters), fairs offered an efficient way to exchange goods, meet new people, and hear news of and see exotic products from far-off places. Today's exquisite annual or biennial antique fairs and weekend flea markets are direct descendants of these fairs.

Though trade increased, material goods were still scarce, and used for longer than they are today. Municipal rubbish collection service did not exist: instead, some items were sold to roving junk dealers. The rest was thrown in the street, where rag pickers and junk men took leftover and discarded goods, sorted through them at home, and salvaged whatever had any value for reuse or resale. The items were sold in the neighbourhoods where the rag pickers lived. One

of the largest and most famous rag pickers'
neighborhoods was just outside the Paris city
walls at the Porte de Saint-Ouen. This area,
especially since World War II, has become what
is probably the largest flea market in Europe,
and possibly in the world.

In large cities such as Calcutta and Cairo,
Manila and Mexico City, rubbish is still disposed
of in a similar way.

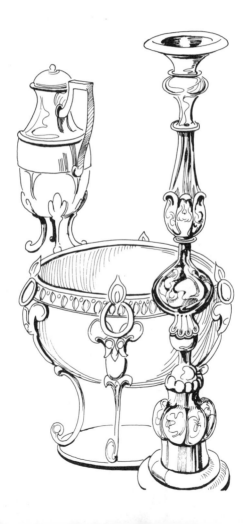

Types of Markets

France's hundreds of markets divide into several types, which are roughly similar to the types of markets in other countries.

You should always try to get a receipt for every purchase. It is needed for Customs when you return home. However, some sellers, especially at flea markets, may be unwilling to give you a written receipt, or will give you an inadequate or illegible receipt. If you can't get an adequate receipt, keep a record of the date, location, description of the item, and price you paid.

Marché aux Puces (Flea Market)

The flea market, especially common in large cities, offers used items and often antiques. Sometimes these are held indoors in semi-permanent or permanent booths, but most often they are held outside or in a public market hall. Dealers may sell new items and reproductions as well as junk and antiques, so check potential purchases carefully.

Marché à la Brocante (Junk Market)

The category of "brocante" includes and centres on old, decrepit items in need of restoration. A vendor of "brocante" at the market implies that the odd miscellany of items all came from his great grandmother's attic in their ancestral farmhouse in the country. A shop selling "brocante" implies dim rooms filled with dusty furniture and other items untouched for decades.

Salon des Antiquaires (Antique Dealers' Salon) sometimes called "Foire des Antiquités" (Antiques Fair)

Vendors at this type of market must be antique dealers, who sell items that come from their shops. Some dealers exclusively work the fairs and shows and do not have shops or warehouses open to the public. However, you can often obtain access to their warehouses by appointment.

Items at fairs are often guaranteed to be antiques; many fairs and salons explicitly ban all reproductions, and have legally certified experts to insure authenticity. Antique fairs (and shops) imply that these wonderful items have been exquisitely cared for, and are equally quite suitable for an elegant chateau, city penthouse, or restored and luxurious manor house.

Auctions

Scope of Auctions

A large proportion of used items and antiques pass through public sales hall auctions. Many bidders are antique dealers, some are collectors, few are foreigners. With a limited number of bidders, most of whom know the territory, auctions often offer much better bargains than shops or antique shows and salons, and often offer a better quality of merchandise than street fairs and flea markets.

In French, auctions are called "les ventes aux enchères".

Where Auctions are Held

Paris

Most important art and antique auctions take place in Paris, at the Hôtel Drouot, the location not far from the Opéra and Grands Boulevards, widely acknowledged as the centre of the French antique trade. The Hôtel Drouot is entirely closed during the month of August.

Here, nestled among hundreds of dealers, you find sales halls, auctioneers' offices, shippers and freight forwarders, consolidators, and experts to study and warrant that the item is as claimed, and who can deal with the French customs and export control agents.

The Provinces

Most French cities and some provincial towns have public auction halls (Salles des Ventes) where auctions are held on a regular basis. When a town has a public auction hall, the usual sale days, addresses, and phone numbers of the hall are included in the detailed town listings.

Finding Auctions and Auction Dates

Most regular auction sales are listed here in the town-by-town section. They can be relied upon, since many have been continuously in business for decades.

Inspection of merchandise and buyer registration is held the day before and the morning of the sale. Often there is no opportunity to inspect items when the sale actually begins, usually at 2 p.m. in the north of France and at 2:30 p.m. in the south.

Special auctions, whether held in Paris or in the provinces, are almost without exception listed in the weekly antique trade newspaper, *La Gazette de l'Hôtel Drouot.*

This publication can be obtained at the Hôtel Drouot, and at some newstands, and through the publisher:

La Gazette de l'Hôtel Drouot
99 rue de Richelieu
75002 Paris
Telephone (1) 42.61.81.78.

Specialized antiques and arts magazines will often have listings announcing special auctions. Coverage in daily and weekly general circulation newspapers will have some information about auctions and antique shows, but they will usually be on a space-available basis and are sometimes incomplete.

How to Participate

Depending on the auctioneer and the auction house, bidding can be as easy as raising your hand or catching the auctioneer's eye with a nod of your head. In other auctions, you may pre-register at the reception desk. In any case, ask at the reception desk before the auction begins.

You will at least need to understand French numbers, to ensure that you know how much you bid. In addition, at least a rudimentary knowledge of French will help. Also, knowledge of the items will be useful; although the auctioneer may describe the items your own knowledge is more reliable.

Payment is in cash, or a cheque drawn in French francs on a French bank with acceptable identification (usually a carte d'identité for French residents, carte de séjour for foreign residents of France, or a passport for non-resident foreigners).

If payment is made with an uncertified cheque, purchases will not be released until the cheque has cleared.

Right to a Receipt

You have the right to receive a written receipt ("le bordereau") for every item you buy at auction. It will be the correct amount, since the auctioneer is legally bound by it. The receipt also is proof of ownership.

Taxes and Commissions

You will be responsible for paying the 6% tax on transfers of antiques, and 17.29% value-added tax ("Taxe sur la Valeur Ajoutée", usually written as TVA) on the sales commission.

You may also have to pay the buyers' premium ("les honoraires des commissaires-priseurs"). This is often which is charged on a sliding scale: for example, at Paris' Hôtel Drouot, the charges on the first 15,000 francs of the purchase are 17.674%, between 15,001 and 40,000 francs are charged 13.2265%, between 40,001 and 300,000 francs are charged 11.151%, and above 300,000 francs are charged 9.965%.

Regulation of Auctioneers and Auctions

French auctions of all types are closely regulated by the government and trade groups. While auctions may be sponsored by various organizations, only a licensed individual auctioneer ("commissaire-priseur") may actually conduct an auction. Auctioneers are personally responsible (and legally liable) for all matters relating to the auctions they conduct.

The trade group, which provides professional standards and from whom information can be obtained and complaints made is:

Compagnie Nationale des Commissaires-
　Priseurs
13 rue de la Grange-Batelière
75009 Paris
Telephone (1) 47.70.89.33.

Who are the Sellers?

You always hope to find friendly, helpful vendors who don't know the value of what they're selling, and therefore will sell it to you for a song. While such sellers do exist, they are only slightly more common than hens' teeth.

Most sellers at flea markets and antique fairs are full-time dealers, who may close their regular shops or leave an assistant to mind the main store. Often, at permanent stands at major full-time flea markets such as Saint-Ouen in Paris, or along Boulevard Risso in Nice, it is the seller's only shop. Depending on the nature of the market, they take either their best or worst items to dispose of—whatever they think will sell.

Dealers' knowledge of their chosen field may vary widely. Many use reference books and price guides to help them keep track of their pricing. The day of the untutored and ignorant seller of antiques has passed almost completely.

Some vendors are junk dealers pure and simple, who drive around in trucks reading (translated) "I buy everything". They clean out basements and attics, old barns, warehouses, and garages. Some even go on early morning safaris looking for salvageable items in the rubbish! Regardless of an item's origin, they may ask the amount listed in the price guides.

Part-time vendors are usually found in strength only at the weekend flea markets where permanent stands aren't available. During the week, they are members of other trades and professions. While many do not have the choicest items, they may be more willing to negotiate and they are often more willing to share experiences. Many of their items may only be of garage-sale or rummage-sale quality.

Many dealers have no fixed place of business, except their vans and trucks, and maybe a dusty barn at their home in the country. They serve as "pickers"—that is, picking up the best around the country, and serving as the city dealers' source of supply. If you can find them before the market opens, they can also serve you as a cheaper source of supply as well. These travelling dealers have the time and patience to seek out house sales, country auctions, and fund-raising sales of charity groups. They often cultivate a grapevine to lead to tips and sources of supply. Because they have no fixed place of business, they often thrive on large turnover and take low markups.

Bargaining

Prices at flea markets and antique fairs are rarely fixed—you can usually obtain reductions of 10 to 50 per cent of the first asking price if you try. Knowing the economics of the market helps.

As a rule of thumb, most dealers try to double the prices of everything they sell. They feel entitled to this for their time, trouble, skill, and luck.

First prices asked almost always include a "fudge factor", since most sellers (and most buyers) expect to haggle and reduce the initial price. In fact, if you fail to bargain, some vendors may be puzzled and deprived of the conversational ritual to set the final price. The conversations as well as the money constitute much of the income many part-time vendors expect and enjoy.

Here are a number of tactics to try to bring the price down:

1. The seller will always make a profit: his or her initial cost is also the base price. Some sellers keep markups low to increase turnover: this will make initial prices seem more reasonable, but there maybe less price flexibility.

If the dealer just obtained the item, the price may be reduced to provide a quick profit to raise cash. The dealer may know of another more desirable object he or she may need some added money to buy. On the other hand, if the item has been a long-time dust collector, and you're the first person even casually interested, the price may be less. If there's been a lot of inflation in the country, the seller may be thinking only of the original price paid.

2. The price is usually on an "as is—where is" basis. If there's an imperfection, use it as a way to try to reduce the price.

3. Bargain even if you know an item is an incredibly good buy. You can still always pay the initial asking price later. Failure to bargain may make the vendor believe that either you're foolish or that the item is very valuable (and it may be withdrawn from sale).

4. Treat sellers as **people** first—this will solve many of your price problems. Politeness, courtesy, and consideration will make a difference.

5. Have at least a basic knowledge of the French language. The ability to communicate is invaluable at the market.

6. When you first see an item you want, set a price on it in your mind even before you pick it up to examine it. Don't pay more if you can help it. The "get it now" mentality used by auctioneers and high-pressure salespeople can lead you to spend far more than you planned. Conversely, there are sometimes a few items you must have, or you'll regret it forever.

7. If you find an item you know is unique, don't wait and plan to come back later. You probably won't, or it will be sold when you do come back. You may never see a similar item again, and be reminded of it every time you see the empty space on your mantelpiece at home.

8. Don't make a beeline for the only item you want. Showing too much interest right off may lead to a higher final price. Better to pick up five or six items of lesser interest, and look at them as well as the items you want.

One manoeuver that sometimes works well is to ask the price of a group of unrelated items, then ask the price of smaller groups, single items, and eventually ask the price of the item you really want.

Often, using this approach, the price of the item you want is less than its proportional share of the whole group—and a bargain besides.

Two Afterthoughts

1. Some dealers are contrary and won't reduce the price at all. It may be only with a particular item, only with foreigners, or the colour of your eyes. This is rare: firm prices are almost unknown at flea markets, and uncommon in fixed antique markets, even in the very exquisite and expensive Louvre des Antiquaires in Paris.

2. Have enough cash to buy what you want. At flea markets, all payments are expected to be cash—in the local currency. No cheques, no credit cards, no foreign money such as sterling.

What Season To Go?

Flea Markets

Flea markets are held year-round in France, just as in the rest of the world. When you go is best determined by other needs, since each season has its special charm. The types of items will not change very much, except that new clothes and fresh vegetables (in those markets that have them) will follow the seasons.

Winter offers fewer markets, somewhat fewer sellers and prospective buyers, and certainly fewer tourists. (Bear in mind, however, that even in winter, you're clearly recognizable as a foreigner, often before you begin speaking.) With fewer buyers, pressure to reduce prices in serious bargaining may be stronger.

Spring is generally more rewarding than winter; not only are people coming out from the cold, but the seasonal flea markets begin to open. Spring cleaning may not be the best known tradition in much of Europe, but longer, warmer, sunnier days bring out more buyers and more sellers as well. Markets open in the morning as the days get longer.

Summer is the high season for the flea market trade. Tourists swarm across the continent; while there are several million from the Britain, the United States, and Canada, and the French themselves outnumber everyone else many times over. Not only do most French workers usually get four or five weeks of paid holiday, they also still follow the tradition of taking this holiday during August.

During the summer season, bargaining may not always bring the lower prices often possible at other times of the year. On the other hand, summer is when many of the smaller, once-a-year countryside fairs and markets take place.

Autumn is in many ways the most rewarding season to search the flea markets. The climate is still relatively mild, the seasonal flea markets are still operating (usually at least until the beginning of November), and most of the tourists have returned home.

Auctions and Fairs

Antique fairs and auctions are held year-round. However, the best shows, sales and fairs usually take place in the autumn, and to a slightly lesser degree in the spring. Fairs in winter tend to be times when dealers stock up for the next spring and autumn.

Language

Don't know a word of French? Don't let that prevent you from going to markets and auctions in France! A surprising number of people speak at least a little English, the international language of commerce. It is required in many secondary schools and universities. Your best chance of finding someone speaking English is with a person of secondary school or college age.

Though knowledge of French gives you a real edge in bargaining, is isn't strictly required for successful flea marketing or purchases at shows. A slightly larger knowledge of French (especially numbers) is necessary at auctions.

You should, however, make an effort to learn at least a few words of French, such as the most important words "please", "thank you", and numbers.

By making the effort to communicate in the seller's native language, you'll engage the seller's sympathy, since they know you've made an effort.

The more you can speak, the more you can ask questions about any particular object, point out its defects, more forcefully haggle over the price, lead the conversation on interesting and price-softening digressions.

If you're a good listener, you'll learn about the item (or at least the range of the seller's knowledge), possibly its history and origin, how (but not usually where) it was found, and other interesting things. As you listen, you'll also get a conversational language course.

The next pages have the basic phrases needed to buy successfully at flea markets, shows, and auctions.

Language Key

Good morning/afternoon	Bonjour
Please	S'il vous plaît
Thank you	Merci
Where is the flea market?	Où est le marché aux puces?
. . . junk market?	. . . le marché de la brocante?
antique fair?	. . . la foire d'antiquités?
. . . crafts market?	. . . le marché artisanal?
Over there	Là bas
Straight ahead	Tout droit
Right. Left	A droit. A gauche
Around the corner	Au coin de la rue
Can you show me on the map?	Pouvez-vous me montrer sur la carte?
At the market	Au marché
How much (does this cost)?	Combien (est-ce)?
That is too much!	C'est trop cher!
What is it?	Qu'est-ce c'est?
How old is it?	Quel âge a-t-il?
How is it used?	Comment est-ce utilisé?
Does it work?	Est-ce que ça marche?
It's broken. Look here!	C'est cassé. Regardez ici!
What is it made out of?	De quoi est-ce fait?
Will you reduce the price?	Pouvez vous réduire le prix?

What is your lowest price?	Quel est le plus bas prix?
Can you take ____ francs?	Acceptez-vous ____ francs?
I don't have enough money.	Je n'ai pas assez argent.
Can I pay with sterling?	Est-ce que je peux payer avec des livres sterling?
I would like a receipt . . .	Je voudrais une facture . .
. . . for our Customs.	. . . pour la douane.
Where are the toilets?	Où sont les toilettes?

```
0 zéro
1 un
2 deux
3 trois
4 quatre
5 cinq
6 six
7 sept
8 huit
9 neuf
10 dix
11 onze
12 douze
13 treize
14 quatorze
15 quinze
20 vingt
30 trente
40 quarante
50 cinquante
60 soixante
70 soixante-dix
80 quatre-vingt
90 quatre-vingt-dix
100 cent
200 deux cents
1,000 mille
2,000 deux mille
5,000 cinq mille
```

Thank you. Goodbye.	Merci. Au revoir.

Market Times and Places

Most antique markets start in midmorning. Most flea markets start very early in the morning. To get a chance at the best of the newly arriving items, you need to arrive at the market as early as the local dealers and collectors. You also need convenient transportation for the specific markets and fairs you want to attend. Transport to weekday central city fairs or auctions calls for a very different transport strategy than a roving tour of country and suburban fairs and markets.

At markets in France, browsers crowd around as the sellers' merchandise is unpacked. The first person to hold a treasure gets the first chance to examine and buy it. Even at the few flea markets (such as Paris' Clignancourt—Porte de Saint-Ouen) where some of the established booths and indoor shops don't open until 9 or 10 in the morning, pavement vendors arrive at dawn—and often leave by the time the indoor stores open and the large crowds arrive. Many times, you'll get better bargains from these early-bird sellers than from dealers in the shops and stalls.

Food, Drink, and Toilets at the Flea Market

Food at the Fair
Most flea markets have food and drink at concession stands. Such convenience food, not noted for quality or good value, ranges from cans of fizzy to small pizzas, sandwiches, hamburgers, chips, as well as a wonderful array of large, domed loaves of country bread, homemade salami, and wines and cider sold by the producer.

Snack food sold at flea markets is usually as safe as any food elsewhere in France. Use the same precautions you would use anywhere.

If the market is part of a general market with fruit and vegetable vendors as well as antiques and junk, you may find better variety and more quality for your money.

Toilets
There are toilets at most markets or in the neighbourhood. They may be primitive, smelly, and ill-maintained. There may not be any toilet paper. Some of the worst ones have attendants to collect money. If no toilets are visible, ask a seller—because they are familiar with the market.

Often facilities for women are unequal to the demand—plan to wait.

In a few major weekend markets in permanent, open-air locations, public toilets may be totally absent. In this case, there may be nearby bars or restaurants where you can find relief. You needn't be a patron—unless you see a sign in the local language that translates to "toilets for patrons only."

Sometimes you'll find a collection plate at a toilet, either public or private. Leave a few small coins (often one franc per use) as the obligation arises. Be sure that you have small change available—no change is given out.

If there are toilets in the area, look for these signs: Toilettes, W.C., Messieurs (Men), Dames (Women).

In a number of markets in open spaces or fields, toilets may be placed in portable trailers. Look for the trailers looming up above the stands. They are often but not always marked.

Transport

Getting to City Markets and Auctions (Weekdays)

The large cities of France have the largest antique markets and usually the largest selection of goods, and are also usually the site of the auction houses. During the week, public transport (underground and buses) may be the the the most economical and convenient way to come and go unless you plan to buy and take bulky items away with you.

Most city markets are crowded; parking space is at a premium. Sometimes illegally parked cars are towed, but less frequently if they are out of the path of traffic.

Parking, whether free or pay, whether on the street or in a garage or a car park, is usually found not too far away from the market. Traffic near a market may be almost at a standstill for hours on end. You can usually walk much faster than you can drive.

French underground systems are closed during the early morning hours: during the week they're closed between 11 p.m. or 1 a.m. and about 5 a.m.

A possible middle course is to park further from the market and take public transport to your destination.

Where information about access via convenient public transport is available, it's included in the description of each flea market.

Getting to City Markets on Weekends

Weekends call for different preferred modes of transport to the market. The bustle of weekday business and work-related traffic subsides, especially on Sunday. Traffic moves more smoothly and rapidly. Parking is much more easily found, often free, and the tow truck drivers and parking-ticket givers often take the day off.

In contrast, public transport often becomes less convenient. The metro and buses revert to a weekend schedule, offering less- frequent service. Weekend service may be infrequent. On weekends, the metro often does not start up until 6 or even 7 a.m., and some stations may close for the entire day. Those at or near markets remain open. Sometimes getting to a Sunday market opening on public transport is impossible. Later in the day, service becomes more frequent, but is rarely up to weekday rush-hour frequency.

Countryside and Suburban Markets

A van or car is almost indispensable for a tour of country markets. Small cities, towns, and villages don't usually have the frequent public transit services found in large cities. Intercity trains don't arrive every five minutes, buses are few and far between, and there is no metro.

French roads are well maintained. Autoroutes (motorways) are well maintained and marked, have high speed limits (maximum 130 kilometers, or about 80 miles per hour). Outside of metropolitan areas, most autoroutes are toll roads, and costs can be high.

Every village is found on the detailed maps published by Michelin. You'll find these maps at bookshops, tourist curio shops, and sometimes garages. (Several oil company sell their own maps at garages though most are less detailed.)

Cars and Vans

Renting a car in France is as easy as in Britain. All you need is your driver's licence and a credit card.

France adds a 28 per cent value-added tax (TVA) to the price of car rentals. You can lease a tax-free vehicle in France if you keep it for at least 21 days and arrange it in advance.

Rentals and leases can be handled from home, before you leave. In addition to major rental companies such as Avis, Hertz and Europcar. If you rent a car in Britain and plan to take it to France, be sure that you're permitted to take it to the Continent, and be sure that you carry proper insurance.

Generally, as a rule of thumb, you can rent a small economy car for less than the cost of two first-class France-Vacances tickets for the same period of time. There are also potential savings on lodging and meals, if you stop in smaller towns and villages. Central city prices are about one-and-a-half times countryside prices for equivalent quality.

Vehicles also offer far greater convenience in keeping your finds at hand rather than leaving them at left-luggage offices at train stations.

If several of you travel together, you can search the market independently, and find the car a convenient meeting place. Each one of you should have a key.

Carrying Your Purchases

When using public transport, you have to carry your purchases with you or send them along by railway express ("service de colis"). Your finds are generally safer when you can carry them with you until you're ready to come home or ship them home.

From this standpoint, a car or van is almost a necessity for serious collectors or dealers on a buying trip. Otherwise, carrying around your treasures can be an exercise of frustration, and cost a fortune in excess baggage, postal, and express shipping charges. Take a hint from the dealers and regular buyers: they don't usually arrive on public transport. They drive.

Carrying Your Finds at Market

Few sellers have adequate, secure, convenient wrapping materials. Most will just hand you the purchased item, possibly wrapped in an old newspaper. Once in a while, a flimsy plastic shopping bag may be available if you ask. These bags are better than nothing, but are lightweight, and can stretch or tear if filled with heavy or sharp-pointed objects.

You're best off bringing your own carrier bag.

Selecting a Market Bag

There is a large variety of carrier bags available. Nylon bags are best: they are strong, light, fold into small places, and shield the contents from the prying eyes of potential thieves. Shoulder straps leave your hands free to inspect items.

Carefully check a bag before you buy it. Look for durability and convenience first rather than style. A good bag has these qualities:

1. The material is strong. Rip-stop nylon is the most durable lightweight fabric. Canvas is heavier (in weight, not strength) and can rot if left in the damp for extended periods.

2. The stitching is strong and seams are secure.

3. The zippers are strong and substantial, and open and close easily.

4. All metal parts are thick and strong: solid brass is best.

If you plan on extensive purchases, take more than one bag with you.

Luggage Carriers

Tourists at very large markets sometimes bring wheeled luggage carriers. They have a number of limitations that make them less useful there than at airports and train stations. Many flea markets have a lot of barriers to the small wheels, such as dirt, gravel, or uneven cobblestone surfaces. Curbs also may interfere with smooth rolling. Many indoor flea markets have stairs that further reduce the utility of these carriers.

Flea markets and antique fairs by their very nature are very crowded, full of jostling people intent on their business. They don't expect to find luggage carriers in their way, and may trip over them.

If you do use a luggage carrier, be sure it is strong and will take a lot of punishing use without breaking. And be sure that the boxes or suitcases can be firmly fastened to the carrier.

String Bags

At one time every store and market had inexpensive string bags for sale. They could fit in a pocket, and seemingly expand to endless degree. Now it is often difficult to find them.

While old-fashioned classic string bags are more compact and portable than nylon bags, they also reveal the contents to the casual observer, and provide less protection against damage.

Export Laws and Licensing

("Protection of the National Cultural Heritage")

France, like most European nations, regulates and restricts export of antiques and artwork considered to be of cultural value. This is to ensure that the "national cultural patrimony" is not lost to foreign countries. In general, the rare, better known, and older items will not be permitted to leave France permanently. When an attempt is made to export an item illegally, it may be confiscated by French customs. Some nations will, under some conditions, assist the French government to recover illegally exported items and return them to France.

Offices in Paris and major provincial cities oversee the rather cumbersome export licensing procedure, which requires approval of the exportation from both French Customs and a museum expert.

Basic Laws

Beginning early in this century, France has amassed a complex web of laws, decrees, and ordinances regulating the protection and export of art objects, antiquities, and collections.

The basic law of 31 December 1913, Article 14, provides for a schedule (list) of items considered of national cultural importance, whether publicly or privately owned. It gives the government the right to inspect, control movement of, and pre-empt sale of any item which has been scheduled. (Generally, only items of outstanding importance are scheduled—and these almost never come up for sale.)

The law of 23 June 1941 generally imposes the export requirements for scheduled items and also for all items falling into a number of protected categories: furniture made before 1830, art objects made before 1900, and all archaeological finds, regardless of age.

The Notice to Exporters published in the Official Gazette issue of 27 February 1949 details the method to obtain an export licence, which has not been substantially changed (and is detailed below).

Additional Notices to Exporters published 24 November 1964 and 30 October 1965 further defined the categories, and states which customs posts must be used in the export of particular types of articles.

Penalties for failure to attempt export without proper papers can result in confiscation of the work(s) and a fine of twice their value.

Classes of Covered Items

Most items may be exported with a proper permit. The following classes of items must have an export licence to be exported. They are found in the customs regulations, called "tarif des douanes".

The regulated classifications are:

- Ex 99.01: Pictures, paintings, and drawings made entirely by the artist's hand, unless the artist is still living or has died in the last 20 years.

- Ex 99.02: Original engravings, prints, and lithographs more than 100 years old.

- Ex 99.03: Original sculptures and statues in any material and medium, unless the artist

is still living or has died in the last 20
years.

- Ex 99.05: Collections of botanical, anatomi-
  cal, and mineral specimens for collections
  unless they are to be used for instructional
  purposes. Coins and medals (or collections of
  them) less than 100 years old are specifical-
  ly excluded from licensing requirements.

- Ex 99.06: Antique objects (defined as items
  over 100 years old) except for musical instruments, books, maps, and all other
  graphic arts.

You must request an export licence for any
items or shipment in any of these categories with
a combined shipment value of over 100,000
Francs.

A request for the export licence must be
accompanied by a list of items you want to
export, with an estimate of the value of each, and
(if possible) a photograph of each.

Requests can be made by you or by an
intermediary and must be made to:

SAFICO (Services des autorisations
financières et commerciales)
42 rue de Clichy
75436 Paris Cedex 09
Telephone (1) 42.81.91.44.

Before the items may be exported, a double
inspection must be made:

First an authorized expert representing the
French museum service (Direction des musées de
France) must inspect the item. These experts
have regular weekly hours when all items must
be made available for inspection. The customs
office you deal with will tell you the date and
location of the museum's inspection office. (In
Paris, this is usually on Wednesday afternoons.)
The museum officials have six months to decide
if an export licence should be granted, though
usually this decision is made much more quickly.
If a licence won't be issued, the museum has the

right to buy the work, or you may decide to keep it in France.

Second, if export is authorized, you will receive the export license (License d'exportation Modéle 02). Then you must fill out a regular export declaration (Déclaration d'exportation, Modéle 1060), and present both forms with the items at one of the designated specialized Customs offices. When inspection has been completed, the items should be exported immediately.

Forfeiture Tax

When items declared to be worth more than 20,000 francs are exported, an export tax of 6% of the value must be paid unless:

1. You are a dealer resident in France.
2. You are a non-resident of France.
3. You are the creator of the work of art.

If the value of the shipment is over 250,000 Francs, you must also ensure that financial arrangements relating to exchange controls are satisfied. Only a bank can arrange this; usually major banks will have specialized offices for this purpose.

If you don't have sales receipts and the value of the shipment is over 250,000 francs, you must ask for a DS export declaration (Déclaration d'exportation modéle DS), also available from SAFICO.

Further information about exports can be obtained at the following centres (English not always spoken):

Centre de Renseignements
Direction Générale des Douanes et Droits
 Indirects
182 rue Saint-Honoré
75001 Paris
Telephone (1) 42.60.35.90.
(This office is conveniently across the square from the Louvre and Louvre des Antiquaires.)

Centre de Renseignements
Direction Générale des Douanes et Droits
　Indirects
1 quai de la Douane (Boîte postale 60)
33024 Bordeaux Cedex
Telephone 45.44.47.10, poste (extension) 153.

Centre de Renseignements
Direction Générale des Douanes et Droits
　Indirects
41 rue Sala (Boîte postale 2353)
60215 Lyon Cedex 02
Telephone 78.43.01.76.

Centre de Renseignements
Direction Générale des Douanes et Droits
　Indirects
4 quai Kléber
67056 Strasbourg Cedex
Telephone 88.32.48.90, poste (extension) 211.

Information can also be obtained from regional offices of the customs service, but the information will not be as complete and reliable as from the above centres. These are available in most large cities: look in telephone books for the regional customs office ("Direction Régionale des Douanes").

A special note on purchases from dealers:

If you buy an antique from a dealer that you believe will fall under the export regulations, and have any suspicion that an export permit will not be granted, you should specify that issuance of an export licence is a condition of sale. Naturally, this is difficult if not impossible for items bought at auctions or at flea markets.

Getting Your Purchases Home

Once you have your antiques and other items, you need to get them home. How you do this depends on many factors: how much there is, its weight and volume, and how soon you need or want it. You have several options: you can take your purchases with you in your car or as as accompanied baggage, ship them by mail, package express, air freight, or for large items, in a shipping crate. If of great volume, you can have purchases shipped in a 20-foot, 40-foot, or 45-foot (jumbo) shipping container or removals lorry.

Bringing Purchases Home with You

By Car

When returning by car, just pack them in your baggage, or put them in a box or carton.

By Air

You can carry your purchases on the plane as hand baggage or check it as baggage. Remember that your baggage is not insured against loss or damage to precious metals, glass and crystal, money, and jewelry.

Baggage Allowances Within Europe

Airlines in Europe accept baggage and charge based on its weight. Each first-class passenger is entitled to 66 pounds (30 kilograms) of checked luggage and one carry-on. Each business and coach passenger is entitled to 44 pounds (20 kilograms) of checked luggage and one carry-on.

The strictness with which the rules are applied will vary between different airlines at the same airport, the same airline at different airports, and even between one airline counter agent and the next.

Excess baggage charges are often steep! The rule of thumb is to charge one per cent of the first-class fare to every kilogram (or fraction), even if you're not in a first-class seat.

Finding Packing Materials

When returning home, pack your purchases so that they will arrive home safely. Surround breakables, and, if available, use plastic bubble-pack or Styrofoam packing peanuts and shells. These materials are available from shipping supply merchants (look under "Emballages" in the Yellow Pages). Sometimes you can find these materials in the early morning along sidewalks in retail areas or the Paris garment district (third arrondissement).

Sturdy cardboard boxes provide excellent protection. Cartons made for shipping household goods (available from moving companies) and those made in China for shipping food (available in early morning before rubbish collection in front of Chinese restaurants and grocery stores) provide the most protection. Almost as durable are cardboard fruit shipping boxes made in France and Italy (available at open air markets and food stores). Those used for apples are very good in size and durability.

Avoid boxes made of a soft grade of cardboard. If you try to fold a corner of a box flap, and it bends easily, cracks, or tears, don't use that box.

Reinforce every cardboard box, especially at seams and corners, with filament tape. Since this tape is not widely available in France, you may want to take a roll with you. Have a sharp knife to cut it—the tape is extremely strong.

Removals by Lorry

If you have bought a large quantity of bulky merchandise, it may be easier to have it brought home by a removals company. In France, look in the Yellow Pages under "Démémagements" and "Transports". Be sure that the company you choose has experience with moving antiques and has experience in making clearing Customs and making deliveries in Britain.

Generally the removals company will also be able to properly pack your purchases.

Clearing British Customs

Customs inspection! The very words can strike terror or great amounts of irritation into many travelers: visions of weary inspectors pawing through your luggage in search of contraband are not pleasant.

What Customs Can Inspect

Every item brought into the United Kingdom from any other country must be made available the Customs for inspection. The if you enter through the Green channel, you may not even see a Customs inspector (unless entering by car). But any customs inspector can decide to nothing, whether a simple suitcase or an entire shipping container. The inspector can decide for any reason, or no reason, to open every package and inspect every item.

The reasons for customs inspection include not only the collection of customs duty and VAT, but also to ensure that all imports are safe, don't violate copyright or trademark laws, and are not prohibited (such as narcotics or items made from endangered species).

In all cases, you should have every bill of sale and receipt readily available to show the customs inspector upon request.

If you have packed goods in boxes, you should have shipping tape, twine, or other materials to reseal the containers when the inspector has finished. While some officers have some tape or other materials available, many do not.

Remember that true antiques are duty free, but the inspector may demand proof.

Duty-Free Allowance

If your purchases of antiques and collectables cost under £250, you can bring in your purchases duty free as part of your baggage.

After that, the inspector will assess duty and VAT as prescribed by regulations: the amount will vary depending on the exact classification of the merchandise.

Formal Entries

For all commercial shipments entering the United Kingdom, you have to go through the Red channel, and make a formal entry.

Whether or not you pass through Customs with your purchases, or have them sent separately, you must follow the prescribed procedure.

1. Provide Customs with an acceptable invoice.

2. Make the goods available for inspection.

3. Pay any duty or VAT that is to be charged.

If you live near the port of entry and want to oversee each step of the process, you can do it yourself. However, you can also hire a customs broker to handle this process for you.

Why Hire a Customs Broker?

Customs brokers are licenced and bonded and can handle all of the details of clearing customs if you can't or don't wish to. Naturally they charge a fee for their services.

When using a broker, you must still play a part by providing a complete commercial or pro-forma invoice and ensure that a complete bill of lading (or airbill) accompanies the shipment. The bill of lading should (if possible) specify the broker who will be clearing the shipment.

Customs brokers cluster around all major ports of entry; they're listed in the Yellow Pages under "Shipping and Forwarding Agents".

How to Select a Broker

Since there may be at least several dozen brokers near most major ports of entry, you need to carefully select the one that will work best for you. Sometimes antique dealers specializing in imported items will tell you which brokers they use, if any (some dealers take care of this themselves).

Ask these questions of any broker you're considering:

1. What experience do you have with antiques and collectables (or type of merchandise you're importing)? How many shipments of such items have you recently cleared?

2. Can you refer me to several recent customers for whom you have cleared this type of merchandise?

3. How much do you charge? Get a breakdown and ask
   • is this fee all inclusive?
   • if not, what extra charges can be added?

Some brokers provide all services for a set price, plus the exact amount of any customs duty payable. Others may have a reasonable base price, plus a charge for every single entry they type on forms and every phone call they make or every paper they handle. There is often no relationship between charges and quality of service.

A knowledgable broker should be able to clear your shipment in just a few days, or even the same day.

Writing and Calling

Writing

Postal Codes and "Départements"

Every French address has a five-digit postal code; its use is the same as the post code of Britain. It is generally written before the name of the town. The first two numbers of the postal code refer to the administrative "département," which is roughly analogous to a county. Most of the approximately 100 départements are named after natural features (most often rivers and mountains). Therefore, there is no pattern to determine what part of France each département occupies.

Writing to French addresses

When writing for information, be sure to put the postal code before the the city name; in large cities, the postal code changes from area to area.

When you see "Cedex" as part of an address be sure to use it. This will send it to a special post office that has only post office boxes.

Telephone Calls

When making a phone call inside Paris or to or from any region of France except Paris (whether local or long distance), just dial the entire eight-digit number. If you are calling to the provinces from Paris or the Paris region, first dial 16, wait for a second dial tone, and then dial the number.

If calling from Paris to the provinces, you must also dial 16 before the number.

Often, telephone numbers in Paris and the Paris region are written showing the prefix (1) to distinguish them from the same number in the provinces.

A complete explanation of using French telephones is found in "Manston's Travel Key Europe", available from the publishers of this book.

Languages Spoken

Often, the tourist office (Office de Tourisme) will have English-speakers. It is somewhat rarer to find a fluent English-speaker at local chambers of commerce have them (Syndicats d'Initiative), since these offices are found in smaller towns. You can't expect that most people you meet at markets, fairs, auctions, offices, and companies will speak English. Generally, younger people recently out of school are most likely to know some English.

Is the Market Going to Be There?

When markets or auctions are held at least once a month, you can expect to find them at the time and place promised. Checking with the listed organizer or information source is not usually necessary. If markets are held less often, it is important to check in advance to confirm the exact dates.

Cities A to X

Agde 34300

Marché de brocante (junk market) every Sunday morning from the beginning of June to mid-September on Quai de la Trinquette and Quai de la Trirème at Cap d'Agde. The market in this newly-created summer resort is interesting; a couple of dozen vendors bring junk including glass, domestic pottery such as jugs and casseroles, and, if you're lucky, pharmacy pots and old drug bottles. Do not confuse the antique market with the Wednesday food market at Parking de la Bulle d'Acceuil, and the Saturday food and clothes market, where few antiques and collectables are to be found. Information from the Office Municipal du Tourisme et des Loisirs, Centre des Congrès, avenue des Sergents, Boîte Postale 544, 34305 Cap d'Agde Cedex, telephone 67.26.38.58, telex 490209 F CAPAGDE, fax 67.21.35.64.

Aigues-Mortes 30220

Foire à la brocante (junk fair) third weekend of June at the foot of the old city walls at Porte de la Gardette. This ancient town, bypassed by the centuries, is on the edge of the windswept Camargue region. The market has typical items of southern France: old copper basins, farm implements, tack (for horses), and, if you're lucky, painted wooden country items. This is one of the major markets in the south of France. Information from M. Delmas, Union des Commerçants et Artisans d'Aigues-Mortes, telephone 66.53.73.47.

Aix-en-Othe 10160

Marché à la brocante (junk market) second Sunday of every month at Le Mineroy. This small, provincial market in Lorraine is full of country items, organised by a recognized authority and antique dealer. Information from M. Robert Richard, Le Mineroy, 10160 Aix-en-Othe, telephone 25.46.72.69.

Aigle 61300

Salon des antiquaires et brocanteurs (antique and junk dealers' salon) Easter weekend and the third weekend of September at the Halle Le Grü. This is a relatively small local fair. Information from the Syndicat d'Initiative, place Fulbert de Beina, 61300 L'Aigle, telephone 33.24.12.40.

Aix-en-Provence 13100

Marché aux puces (flea market) Tuesday, Thursday, and Saturday from 8 a.m. to 1 p.m. year round at the place de Verdun facing the Palais de Justice. The setting is one of the most picturesque in France, and the 20 or 30 vendors of antiques and collectables offer good variety. This market offers a lot of porcelain and some faience, much silver and silver plate, books, and some crystal. There is only a small quantity of furniture. A few vendors have spilled over into the adjoining place de Precheurs, which is mainly a food market. The food market displays the agricultural plenty of Provence, especially late in summer, when the melons from nearby Cavaillon share top billing with tomatoes and peaches. There are no toilets at the market. Parking is difficult in this congested, ancient area. Pay parking garages are found a short distance away at place Bellegarde, and also along boulevard Saint-Louis. Information from the Office du Tourisme, place Général de Gaulle, 13100 Aix-en-Provence, telephone 42.26.02.93.

Salon des antiquaires (antique dealers' salon) second half of November (exact dates change from year to year) at the Salle Carnot, 14 place Carnot. This salon is full of Provençal artisans' work and a has a good selection of antiques. This is one of the larger annual markets in the south of France. Organised by the M. Bouzon, Syndicat des Antiquaires Aixois, 13 rue Granet, 13100 Aix-en-Provence, telephone 42.26.02.93 or 42.23.16.86.

Aix-les-Bains 73100

Exposition-vente d'antiquités (antiques exposition and sale) first Friday to following Monday in October in the Palais des Fleurs on rue Jean Monard. This is a small regional sale in a famous old thermal resort. Information from the Commission d'Animation du Palais des Fleurs, rue Jean Monard, 73100 Aix-les-Bains, telephone 42.26.02.93.

Ajaccio (Corsica) 20000

Marché aux puces (flea market) every Sunday morning from 7 a.m. to 1 p.m. at the Marché Central (central market hall) right in the centre of town along the boulevard du Roi Jérôme facing the city gardens. This lively market, which is part of the general market offering food and new items, mainly offers junk and regional specialities such as copper cauldrons, old armaments left over from the feuding days, and Napoleonic souvenirs. On Saturday mornings, the market takes place on Cours Grandval, in the town centre facing the city gardens. Information from the Agence Régional de Tourisme (closed Saturday and Sunday), 22 cours Granval, 20000 Ajaccio, telephone 95.51.00.22.

Albi 81000

Marché aux puces (flea market) every Saturday morning year round on place Lapérouse, just near the old town centre, with its narrow, picturesque, and twisting streets. You may find regional items such as copper basins, folk art, domestic pottery such as plain clay wine pitchers and platters. Parking garages are available in the neighbourhood on boulevard Général Sibille, not too far from the cathedral. Information from the Office de Tourisme, Palais de la Berbie, place Saint-Cecile, 81000 Albi, telephone 63.54.22.30, telex 533404 F OTSI.

Foire à la brocante et aux antiquaires (junk and antique dealers' fair) first weekend of October. This is a regional fair of between 50 and 100 dealers. Organised by C.F.E.A., 14 rue Timbal, 81000 Albi, telephone 63.54.67.19.

Alençon 61000

Salon d'automne d'antiquités et de brocante (autumn antique and junk salon) the end of October and beginning of November. This is a relatively small regional fair, held indoors at the Parc des Expositions. Information from the Parc des Expositions, Boîte Postale 109, 61004 Alençon Cedex, telephone 33.26.23.98.

Amboise 37400

Salon d'antiquités (antiques salon) during the first half of July (centreing on July 14, which is Bastille Day) at the Grange de Négron. This small regional fair doesn't offer large size or distinctive items, but is often crowded with summer tourists. Information from Mme. Huauly, 12 rue Nationale, 37400 Amboise.

Amiens 80000

Marché aux puces (flea market) every Saturday morning year round at place Henriette Dumuin. This market in the level northern region of France is part of the weekly general merchandise and food market. Dozens of vendors turn out on the few sunny days; in inclement weather there are fewer, selling regional speciality items including faience, household copper ware, and beer pitchers and mugs. Information from the Office de Tourisme, Maison de la Culture, rue Jean Catelas, 80000 Amiens, telephone 22.91.79.28.

Angers 49000

(Please also see Durtal 49430.)

Marché aux puces (flea market) Saturday from early morning to about noon year round at place Louis Imbach. The setting is wonderful: quaint old buildings surround this tree-shaded, irregularly-shaped square. Though over 100 sellers are at this mixed market, many sell only new items and food. This market has a fair amount of used furniture (less on rainy days) plus normal flea-market items such as glass, crystal, porcelain, tarnished silver plate (and a little solid silver). Public toilets are available. Street parking is difficult, since during the rest of the week the square is the neighbourhood car park. Information from the Mairie d'Angers, Service des droits de place, boulevard du Marüchal Foch, 49000 Angers, telephone 41.86.10.10.

Broc et puces (junk fair) the last weekend of April at Parc Expo. This is a relatively new fair, and complements the fall fair at Durtal. For more information, contact Angers Parc Expo, telephone 41.93.40.40 or 41.90.42.65.

Salle des Ventes (public sales hall) auction every Tuesday at 2 p.m. Information and buyer registration is held before the market begins. Information from the Salle des Ventes, 52 rue du Maine, 49000 Angers, telephone 41.60.55.19.

Marché aux fleurs (flower market) every Saturday morning at place Bessonneau, in the central city area. This market sells mostly flowers, not antiques and collectables. Information from the Mairie d'Angers, Service des droits de place, boulevard du Marüchal Foch, 49000 Angers, telephone 41.86.10.10.

Foire aux croûtes et é la brocante (crust and junk fair) third Sunday of March on the rue des Lices, from early morning until late afternooon. For information, contact M. Froger, Association pour l'animation de la rue des Lices, 29 rue des Lices, 49000 Angers, telephone 41.87.42.01.

Angoulême 16000

Marché aux puces (flea market) third Sunday of the month year round at place Saint-Martial in the centre of this fascinating old walled city. This is one of the more interesting regional flea markets, with dozens of vendors. Specialities of the region include copper ware and faience, and rustic farm furniture and implements. Street parking is difficult in the narrow streets, but there is a garage near the city hall. Information from the Office de Tourisme, 2 place Saint-Pierre, Boîte Postale 222, 16007 Angoulême Cedex, telephone 45.95.16.84, telex 792215 F.

Salon des antiquaires (antique dealers' salon) the first Friday to following Monday of December (may include the last day of November) at the Logis de Lunesse. This fair is where about 60 regional dealers show furniture, copper, and faïence. Information from M. Fragne, 8 rue Ludovic Trarieux, 16000 Angoulême, telephone 45.95.62.42.

Annecy 74000

Marché aux puces (flea market) last Saturday of every month year round on flowered banks of the Thiou river in the city centre and along the lake. This is one of the most picturesque markets in France; you may find regional speciality items including wooden butter moulds and primitive folk art and wood carving, household items, and occasionally heavy rustic furniture and painted farm furniture. Information from the Service des Affaires Economiques, Boîte Postale 305, 74000 Annecy, telephone 50.33.65.54.

Salon d'antiquités de la rentrée (antiques and collectors' salon) at the end of August and first few days of September at the Parc des Expositions. About 100 exhibitors (mainly dealers) display their wares, which include furniture, wood items, and occasional silver pieces. The first two days (always Thursday and Friday) are reserved for dealers—bring your business card and maybe a copy of your business licence or tax registration certificate). There is no entry fee for dealers, but there is an admission charge for the public. Information from the Parc des Expositions, 74000 Annecy, telephone 50.45.01.04, or the Groupement Savoisien, 4 rue Jean-Jaurès, 74000 Annecy, telephone 50.45.56.52.

Les antiquaires de l'Emeraude (antique dealers of Emeraud), every day except Sunday and Monday morning at 4 rue Jean Jaurès. This building contains about 25 dealers, offering items such as 18th- and 19th-century furniture, Art Deco knicknacks, lamps, and furniture, and other items. Pay parking is available at place de la Préfecture and also the Parking de Bonlieu (along the avenue d'Albigny).

Annet 77410

Marché aux puces (flea market) second Sunday of every month year round at 15 rue du Mancel. This is a small flea market near the western edge of the Parisian suburbs. The selection runs to cut glass, crystal, bronzes, and other items usually found in Paris. However, few of the best items are found at this market.

Annonay 07100

Marché aux puces (flea market) second Sunday of the month year round at the place de la Libération. This is a small market in a poor area. Prices will be lower than in major cities, and rustic items predominate. Information from Mme. Barbato, Bureau de Tabacs, 40 rue Boissy d'Anglas, 07100 Annonay, telephone 75.33.00.06.

La foire-exposition du Haut-Vivarais (exposition and fair of the upper Vivarais) takes place every year at the parc de la Lombardière on Ascension weekend. Some antiques and junk are offered. Information from Chambre de Commerce et d'-Industrie, parc des Platanes, 07100 Annonay.

Antibes 06600

Marché aux puces (flea market) Thursday and Saturday mornings at the place Audiberti. This is an interesting but relatively touristed market. Organised by Service d'Animation Economique Communale, Halles et Marchés, Mairie d'-Antibes, B.P. 2205, 06606 Antibes Cèdex, telephone 93.34.48.66. Information is also available from M. Gismondi, Association des Commerçants, artisans, et artistes forains du Viel Antibes, 14 rampe des Saleurs, 06600 Antibes, telephone 93.34.65.65.

Salon des antiquaires (antique dealers' salon) two weeks at Easter (the end of March and/or early April) during daylight hours on the yacht harbor's edge at Port Vauban. A large car park near the port is free to salon patrons. Information from M. Gismondi, Association des Commerçants, artisans, et artistes forains du Viel Antibes, 14 rampe des Saleurs, 06600 Antibes, telephone 93.34.65.65.

Apt 84400

Foire à la brocante (junk fair) last Saturday of July to the following Tuesday in the town centre. About 100 private collectors, junk and antique dealers offer, in addition to normal flea market items, rustic Provençal furniture, possibly even a few minor paintings. Information from the Office de Tourisme, avenue Philippe de Girard, Bîte Postale 15, 84400 Apt, telephone 90.74.03.18, or from the organiser, M. Albert Gassier, Boîte Postale 45, 84800 L'Isle-sur-Sorgue, telephone 90.38.10.43.

Arcachon 33120

(Please see Teich.)

Argenteuil 95100

Marché aux puces (flea market) every Sunday morning year round on boulevard Héloïse and the adjoining Promenade Gabriel-Peri. Several dozen vendors offer items such as minor faïence and porcelain, bistro glassware, lamps, milk pitchers, et cetera. Since this market is in a suburb of Paris, expect Parisian quality in the displayed items, and Parisian prices to match.

Arles 13200

Marche aux puces (flea market) Saturday morning year round from dawn to about noon on boulevard des Lices, and straggling along part way down boulevard Victor Hugo. During the week the wide shoulders of the boulevard are car parks; on Saturday they sprout hundreds of vendors, mostly of food. This is one of the liveliest markets in France, rain or shine. The dozen to two dozen antique and junk dealers congregate on the small path in the small park leading up to rue Vauban. Only small amounts of furniture are brought to this market, but there is often a lot of good-quality silver plate and crystal. The rest of the market includes squawking caged chickens and cooing doves, vegetable and fruit vendors, and bakers' products including round, domed country breads baked in wood-fired ovens.

Arles is also the centre of the olive-wood carving area, though few of these products are found at the market. These graceful free-form bowls are new, becoming scarce, and not cheap, but are not found anywhere else in the world. Public toilets are in the park, but are poorly maintained. Parking is very difficult—plan to park a short distance away and walk. Information from Mairie d'Arles, place de la République, 13200 Arles, telephone 90.93.98.10.

Salon des antiquités et de la brocante (antiques and junk dealers' salon) last week of September (two weekends and the week between them) from 10 a.m. to 7 p.m. at the Palais des Congrès on the bank of the Rhone river on avenue Président Allende. The Friday before the public opening is reserved for members of the trade. About 60 dealers bring extensive quantities of antiques, furniture, and collectables to this fair. Information from M. Raymond Maurin, 4 rue de Grille, 13200 Arles, telephone 90.96.51.57.

Aubagne 13400

Marché mensuel de brocante et de l'artisanat (monthly junk and handicraft market) the last Sunday of the month at the Gros de la Tourtelle. This is the largest flea market in the vicinity of Marseille, and is also relatively free of tourists. Information from the Syndicat d'Initiative, esplanade de Gaulle, 13400 Aubagne, telephone 42.03.49.98.

Auch 32000

Marché aux puces (flea market) second Saturday of every month from November to June round from early morning until about 4 p.m. at the Maison de Gascogne and market hall across the street from the post office. There is no admission charge. Information is available from the Syndicat d'Initiative d'Auch, 1 rue Dessoles, Boîte 83, 32003 Auch Cedex, telephone 62.05.22.89.

Salon des antiquaires et floralies (antique dealers' and flower salon) the third weekend of October at the Hall du Mouzon. Here you'll find Gascon specialities such as pottery, copper basins, farm furniture, cast iron ware, and old bottles. This is one of the more interesting markets in southern Frnce. Information is available from the Syndicat d'Initiative d'Auch, 1 rue Dessoles, Boîte 83, 32003 Auch, telephone 62.05.22.89.

Aumale 76390

Foire à la brocante (junk fair) third Sunday of May and third Sunday of October (starts early) at the place des Marchés and adjoining Halle au Beurre, northeast of the town centre. This relatively small regional market may yield odds and ends from the north country and Normandy. Information from the Syndicat d'Initiative, rue Centrale, 76390 Aumale.

Aurillac 15000

Marché aux puces (flea market) first Saturday of the month year round in the Quartier des Alouettes, near the regular food and general market. This market is rather small and unsophisticated, relatively strong on folk art as would be expected in a never-prosperous region in the mountainous centre of France. Information from the Office de Tourisme, place Square, 15000 Aurillac, telephone 71.48.46.58.

Auxerre 89000

Salle des Ventes (public sales hall) auction every Friday at 2 p. m. Expect to see heavy Burgundian furniture (especially from the 19th century) farm tables, faïence, rugs, and occasional tapestries, silver tastevins (wine tasting cups), and more. Twice a year, there are sales of antiquities and archaeological items from the Egyptian, Greek, Roman and Asian civilizations. Information and sales at the Salle des Ventes, 21 avenue Pierre-Larousse, 89000 Auxerre, telephone 86.52.17.98.

Salon des antiquaires (antique dealers' salon) in mid-October at the Parc des Expositions. This is a local antiques fair. For exact dates and further information, contact M. C. Dumielle, 1 rue Nicolas Maure, 89000 Auxerre, telephone 86.52.33.93.

Avignon 84000

(Please also see L'Isle-sur-la-Sorgue and Villeneuve-les-Avignon.)

Marché de brocante (junk market) every Saturday year round from 7:30 a.m. to 6 p.m. (closed

12:30 to 2:30 p.m.) at place Crillon, on the Rhone bank, at the main bridge (Pont Edouard Daladier). This market often has local items such as old winemaking items and bottles, local pottery, hand-blown glass, and, very rarely, carved olivewood. Twice a year, the last weekend of May and last weekend of August, the market becomes much larger and spills out along the riverbank allées des Oulles. Information from the Office de Tourisme, 41 cours Jean-Jaurès, 84000 Avignon, telephone 90.82.65.11, or (for the May and October fairs) from the organiser, M. Albert Gassier, O.R.S.E.F., Boîte Postale 45, 84800 L'Isle-sur-Sorgue, telephone 90.38.10.43.

Petit marché aux puces (little flea market) every Sunday morning from 8 a.m. to 1 p.m. at the place des Carmes, east of central square and Palace of the Popes. This fine tree-shaded square faces the Saint-Symphorien Church. The market has about 30 regular dealers. However, finds are less likely than at the Saturday market because this market is better known. Organised by the Cabinet des Adjoints, Ville d'Avignon, 84022 Avignon Cedex. Information from the Office de Tourisme, 41 cours Jean-Jaurès, 84000 Avignon, telephone 90.82.65.11.

Salon des antiquaires (antique dealers' salon) second or third week of February at the Palais des Expositions. You will find dozens of dealers from the region and a lot of Provençal furniture. Information from the Office de Tourisme, 41 cours Jean-Jaurès, 84000 Avignon, telephone 90.82.65.11.

Marché d'un jour reservés aux professionels (one-day market reserved for professionals) four times a year in mid-February, beginning of June and September, and in mid- to late November from 8 a.m. until 8 p.m. (for all practical purposes is over by 2 p.m.) at the Parc des Expositions on Route Nationale 7. These are some of the largest one-day fairs in France, with over 450 vendors. Because this fair is reserved for the trade, a business card or copy of a business licence is necessary for entry. Organised by M. Albert Gassier,

O.R.S.E.F., Boîte Postale 45, 84800 L'Isle-sur-Sorgue, tel. 90.38.10.43.

Foire à la brocante (junk fair) twice a year for four days near Pentecost (early in the year and the beginning of September. These large fairs move from location to location; contact the organiser for exact dates and place. For information, contact M. Jean-Pierre Mahieu, O.R.S.E.F., Boîte Postale 45, 84800 L'Isle-sur-Sorgue, tel. 90.38.17.44.

Hôtel des Ventes (public sales hall) auction every Thursday at 9 a.m. and two Sundays per month at 2.30 p.m. This is one of the larger regular auction sales; often you can find rustic Provençal armoires, buffets, and marriage chests. This auction hall also has occasional auctions of better-quality, specialized items. Advance catalogues are available, and these special sales are announced in the Gazette de l'Hôtel Drouot. Inspection and buyer registration are held the day before the sale. Information and sales at the Hôtel des Ventes, 74 bis rue Guillaume Puy, 84000 Avignon, telephone 90.86.35.35.

Additional street markets, which always seem to include a few antique and junk dealers among the vendors of fruit, vegetables, clothes, and other odds and ends are found at:

- avenue Trillade, every Wednesday, outside the south city walls, under and past the railroad tracks along the airport road. Information from the Office du Marchés, Hôtel de Ville, 84000 Avignon, telephone 90.82.99.00.

- Le Rocade, first Wednesday and Sunday of the month. Information from the Office du Marchés, Hôtel de Ville, 84000 Avignon, telephone 90.82.99.00.

- avenue Colchester in the Saint-Jean district every Thursday year round. Information from the Office du Marchés, Hôtel de Ville, 84000 Avignon, telephone 90.82.99.00.

- place J.-P. Rameau every Saturday morning. Information from the Office du Marchés, Hôtel de Ville, 84000 Avignon, telephone 90.82.99.00.

Barjac 30430

Foires de Barjac (Barjac fairs) Easter Sunday and the following Monday, August 12-15 (Assumption Day holiday) and the post card fair on the first Saturday and Sunday of January after New Years' Day at the Mas de Jurande. These fairs in the hills of the Midi in south-central France prohibit sales of reproductions. Regional dealers predominate, offering folk art, old copper, and country furniture. These are major fairs and well worth attending. Organised by the Comité d'Expansion, Mas de Jurande, 30430 Barjac, telephone 66.52.42.39 or 66.60.50.65.

Bar-le-Duc 55000

Salon des antiquaires (antique dealers' salon) usually the second week of September at the Hall des Expositions on rue Gambetta. The show is one of the oldest in France; here is a place to find antique glass (pre-1900), paintings and prints, and fine 18th-century wooden furniture from the province of Lorraine. Since it is widely announced in the European antique trade press, you'll find buyers from all over northern Europe. Information from M. Moes, Office de Tourisme, 12 rue Lepique, Boîte Postale 211, 55005 Bar-le-Duc Cedex, telephone 29.79.11.13.

Bastia (Corsica) 20200

Marché aux puces (flea market) Sunday year round until 1 p.m. at place Saint-Nicholas in the town centre. This market offers some folk items from Corsica's past. Parking is available in underground garages directly under the market location. Information from the Office de Tourisme, 33 boulevard Paoli, 20200 Bastia, telephone 95.31.02.04, or at place Saint-Nicholas, telephone 95.31.00.99.

Bayeux 14400

Salle des Ventes (public sales hall) auctions some Saturdays (occasionally also on Sunday) at 2:30 p.m. Public inspection and buyer registration is the morning of the sale. Street parking is difficult; there are two paying car parks at the end of the street. Information and sales at the Salle des Ventes, 7 rue des Bouchers, 14400 Bayeaux, telephone 31.92.04.47.

Bayonne 64100

Marché aux puces (flea market) every Friday from 8 a.m. to 12 p.m. at the Halles Municipales Soumoulou. Several dozen vendors are always at this market, which is far larger on the first Friday of every month, and also on the first Sunday of every month. You won't find much furniture (since much Basque furniture consists of massive armoires, farm tables, and marriage chests) but there's a good amount of faïence from Samadet, and locally fired clay jugs for water and oil. Information from the Office de Tourisme, place de la Liberté, 64100 Bayonne, telephone 59.59.31.31.

Beaune 21200

Village des antiquaires (antique dealers' village) open every day except Sunday at 21 boulevard Saint-Jacques. Ten dealers have permanent shops in this indoor arcade and charge high prices for furniture, art objects, etc. These merchants give sizable trade discounts to dealers; bring a business card or copy of a business licence. Information from the same address, telephone 80.22.61.30.

Belfort 90000

Marché aux puces (flea market) first Sunday of every month year round from 8 a.m. to 1 p.m. in the city centre. This is a relatively small market in the southeast of France. Since local cultural influences are from neighboring Alsace and Franche-Comte; you'll find items from both areas, but there don't seem to be many local specialities. Organised by the Ville de Belfort, Service des Marchés, Hôtel de Ville, place d' Armes, 90000 Belfort, telephone 84.28.12.23.

Salon aux antiquités (antiques salon) the third weekend of June at the Patinoire (ice skating rink). This is the only regional fair in the area. For exact information, telephone the organisers at 84.28.17.56.

Benfeld 67230

(Please also see Obernai and Strasbourg.)

Marché aux puces (flea market) Saturdays from 10 a.m. to noon and 2 to 7 p.m. This indoor flea market is the permanent home to about 20 dealers, plus assorted vendors outside. This market is right on R.N. 83, the main road between Strasbourg and Colmar.

Bergerac 24100

Marché aux puces (flea market) first Sunday of every month year round. This small market is held as part of the much larger Sunday food and general market. Information from the Office de Tourisme, 97 rue Neuve d'Argenson, 24100 Bergerac, telephone 53.57.03.11.

Hôtel des Ventes (public sales hall) auctions every Wednesday and Sunday, plus irregular special sales of high- quality goods. Special sales are announced in the Gazette de l'Hôtel Drouot, and have a catalogue. Inspection and buyer registration is held before the sale begins. Sales and information from Hôtel des Ventes, 13 place

Gambetta, 24100 Bergerac, telephone
53.57.38.16.

Bernay 27300

Salon des antiquaires (antique dealers' salon)
Easter weekend on rue de l' Abbatiale in the
centre of town. This is a local fair. Information
from M. Cheron, 25 rue Gaston Folloppe, 27300
Bernay, telephone 32.43.05.47.

Salle des Ventes (public sales hall) auctions on
some weekends. Contact the auction house for
exact dates and conditions of sale. Sales are held
at the Salle des Ventes, route d'Orbec, 27300 Bernay, telephone 32.43.47.41.

Besançon 25000

Petit marché a la brocante (little junk market)
every Friday and Saturday morning year round
(better on Saturday) at the place de la Revolution
in the centre of town in front of the entrance to
the fine arts museum (which has an excellent
collection of clocks and time pieces). The antique
section of this food and general-items market has
only about half-a-dozen vendors, who offer many
reproductions and few antiques. Information
from the Office de Tourisme, place de la 1re
Armée Française, 25041 Besançon Cedex,
telephone 81.80.92.55, telex 360242 F.

Marché aux puces (flea market) second Sunday
of every month year round (except not in July,
August, and September) from 8 a.m. to 1 p.m. at
the Parc des Expositions on rue du Docteur-
Mouras, about three kilometres out of town along
Route Nationale 73, almost at the bypass road in
the Saint-Ferjoux district. This is the best flea
market in the area, with about 40 vendors, but
much larger in June, when it becomes a large
regional fair called the "Foire à la brocante".
You'll find watches, clocks, arms, and, sometimes, exquisite fruitwood carvings and massive
copper cauldrons. Information from the Parc des
Expositions et des Congrès, rue du Docteur

Mouras, Boîte Postale 2019, 25050 Besançon Cedex, telephone 81.52.73.53.

Salon Comtois des antiquaires (Franche-Comte antique dealers' salon) first week of October from about 10 a.m. to 8 p.m. at the Parc des Expositions et des Congrès. This is on rue du Docteur-Mouras, about 3 kilometres out of town along Route Nationale 73, almost at the bypass road in the Saint-Ferjoux district. This is one of the major antique shows of France, with around a hundred dealers showing exquisite clocks, jewellery, and furniture. An admission fee is charged, but there is ample parking on the grounds. Information from M. Coudurier, Parc des Expositions et des Congrès, rue du Docteur Mouras, Boîte Postale 2019, 25050 Besançon Cedex, telephone 81.52.73.53, or from the organisers, Groupe des Salons Selectionées, boulevard de Champagne, Boîte Postale 108, 21003 Dijon Cedex, telephone 80.71.44.34.

Béziers 34500

Marché aux puces (flea market) Friday morning (early!) year round at place de 14-Juillet (Champ de Mars). The market site is about 500 metres east of the allées Paul Riquet; go on avenue George Clemenceau to the post office, and then turn right at that corner and go for one block. The market is across the street, avenue J. Moulin. Parking can be difficult. This is one of the better markets in the south of France: sometimes you can find 19th-century glass, jewelry, and silver (or silver plate), old pharmacy pots and medicine jars, wine-growing tools, and other odds and ends. This is a long-established market, located in a large enough city to have a good selection. Information from the Office de Tourisme, Hôtel du Lac, 27 rue Quatre-Septembre, 34500 Béziers, telephone 67.49.24.19.

Salle des Ventes (public sales hall) auction at irregular intervals throughout the year; contact the auction house for exact dates and further information. Information and sales are held at the

Salle des Ventes, 59 avenue Président Wilson, 34500 Béziers, telephone 67.62.20.14.

Blois 41000

Marché régional de la brocante (regional junk market) the second Sunday of every month year round from 7 a.m. to 6 p.m. in the old centre of Blois on rue Jeanne d'Arc, place Avé-Maria, and in the pedestrian precinct. This market brings some of the better items of the central Loire valley, including massive copper, rustic faïence ware, old muskets, powder horns, and other hunting items, and glassware. The market is moderate in size; only sometimes will you make a find. Organised by the Comité d'Animation du Vieux Blois, at telephone 54.78.45.76. Information from the Office de Tourisme, Pavillion Anne de Bregtagne, 3 avenue Jean-Laigrette, 41000 Blois, telephone 54.74.06.49.

Salon des antiquaires (antique dealers' salon) the third week of October in the quartier des Jacobins. This is a local fair. For information contact M. Habert, 14 rue des Jacobins, telephone 54.78.13.77.

Bolbec 76210

Hôtel des Ventes (public sales hall) auction two Saturdays per month (call for exact dates), starting at 2 p.m. Inspection of merchandise and buyer registration in the day before the sale and the morning of the sale. You're likely to find large, heavy, dark provincial furniture favoured in Normandy, cider mugs, glassware of the 19th century (both cut and painted), and more. Information and sales at the Hôtel des Ventes, 37 rue Gambetta, 76210 Bolbec, telephone 35.31.06.53.

Bordeaux 33000

Marché à la brocante (junk market) Monday to Friday from 8 a.m. to 6 p.m. and Sundays and holidays from 8 a.m. to about 1 p.m. at place

Meynard in the Saint-Michel district, south of the city centre. This market is part of a large food and general market; all of the vendors are full-time dealers. Parking is difficult but available at the market halls. Information from the Office de Tourisme, 12 cours 30-Juillet, 33000 Bordeaux, telephone 56.44.28.41, telex 570362 F, or Accueil de France at the Saint- Jean railway station, telephone 56.91.64.70, or at the the airport, telephone 56.34.39.39.

Marché à la brocante (junk market) Thursday year round from 8 a.m. to 1 p.m. at place Saint-Pierre, in the old city centre not far from the river. Several dozen vendors offer antiques, junk, and modern crafts and sometimes modern art. Information from the Office de Tourisme, 12 cours 30-Juillet, 33000 Bordeaux, telephone 56.44.28.41.

Hôtel des Ventes (public sales hall) auction every Tuesday, Wednesday, and Thursday at 2 p.m. Inspection of sale items and buyer registration is held before the auction begins. All types of furniture, used items, and some antiques are sold at one of the largest auctions in southwestern France. Information and sales at the Hôtel des Ventes, 29 rue de Cheverus, 33000 Bordeaux, telephone 56.44.20.46.

Hôtel des Ventes (public sales hall) auction every Thursday year round at 2.30 p.m. Inspection of sale items and buyer registration is held before the auction begins. Information and sales at the Hôtel des Ventes, 40 cours du Médoc, 33000 Bordeaux, telephone 56.39.28.68.

Salon des antiquaires Bordeaux-Lac (Bordeaux antique dealers' salon) second week of February at the Parc des Expositions, about 3 kilometres north of the city center on the main through road leading to the Pont d'Aquitaine suspension bridge. Several hundred exhibitors show fine antiques, including 18th- and 19th-century paintings, sculpture, silver, and elegant furniture as well as wine paraphernalia. This is an important fair, with high quality antiques. Information from M. Goulignac, Salon des Antiquaires du

Sud-Ouest, 6 rue des Remparts, 33000 Bordeaux, telephone 56.81.80.88.

Salon des antiquaires de Bordeaux-Laîné (Bordeaux antique dealers' salon) in mid-January at the Laîné-Bordeaux warehouse. Information from the Chambre Syndicate des Antiquaires et Brocanteurs, 15 rue Bouffard, 33000 Bordeaux, telephone 45.44.26.64.

Bouchamps-les-Craon 53400

Foire à la brocante (junk fair) the weekend of August 14 at the municipal grounds of this tiny village. This is a local fair, with few visitors from outside the region. For information contact M. Hamard, Bouchamps-les-Craon, 53800 Renaze, telephone 43.06.47.54.

Bourg-en-Bresse 01000

Foire à la brocante (junk fair) third Saturday of every month at the place Jerome Lalande, between the rue d'Espagnel and the avenue Alsace-Lorraine in the town centre. On other Saturdays this is strictly a food market. For information, contact the Office de Tourisme, 6 avenue Alsace-Lorraine, 01000 Bourg-en-Bresse, telephone 74.22.49.40.

Salon des antiquaires (antique dealers' fair) second and third week of September at the Parc des Expositions et de Loisirs on the route Point d'Ain. This is a major regional fair. Information (and exact dates) from the Parc des Expositions, route de Pont d'Ain, 01000 Bourg-en-Bresse, telephone 74.22.12.33.

Hôtel des Ventes (public sales hall) auctions held at irregular intervals. For exact dates and further information, contact sales hall at Hôtel des Ventes, 51 rue Debeney, 01000 Bourg-en-Bresse, telephone 74.83.30.18.

Bourges 18000

Marché de la brocante (junk market) second Sunday of the month from April to November. This is a small market whose location is changeable. Information from the Foire de Bourges, Palais des Congrès, boulevard Lamarck, 18000 Bourges, telephone 48.70.11.22, or the Maison de Tourisme, 21 rue Victor Hugo, Boôte Postale 145, 18000 Bourges, telephone 48.24.75.33.

Journées de l'antiquité (antique days) the second weekend of February at the Parc des Expositions near the canal. This small fair is held indoors. A large car park is on the site. Organised by the Palais des Congrès, telephone 48.70.11.22. Information from the Service des Manifestations Commerciales, Maison de Tourisme, 14 place E. Dolet, 18000 Bourges, telephone 48.24.75.33.

Bourron-Marlotte 77780

Marché aux puces (flea market) every Saturday and Sunday morning at the Pavé du Roy. This is a small local market.

Brest 29200

Foire à la brocante (junk fair) the first weekend of March from early morning to midafternoon at the Parc de Penfeld. This is a large regional fair. Information from the Office de Tourisme, place Liberté, Boôte Postale 24, 29266 Brest, telephone 98.44.24.96.

Hôtel des Ventes (public auction hall) auction every Tuesday at 2 p.m. and on Tuesday nights at 7 p.m. Inspection and registration is held before the sale begins. Information is available from and sales are held at Hôtel des Ventes, 26 rue du Château, 29200 Brest, telephone 98.80.50.53.

Brive-la-Gaillarde 19100

Marché aux puces (flea market) first and third Tuesday of every month year round on cours Martignac. The market is small and the choice is sometimes very limited. Information from the Office de Tourisme, place 14-Juillet, 19100 Brive-la-Gaillarde, telephone 55.24.08.80.

Salle des Ventes (public sales hall) auction every Saturday year round at 2 p.m. Inspection and buyer registration is held before the sale. Information and sales at the Salle des Ventes, 7 rue Vincent-Chassaing,   19100   Brive-la-Gaillarde, telephone 55.24.11.12.

Cabourg 14390

(Please   also   see   Caen,   Deauville,   and Dives-sur-Mer.)

Foire d'antiquités et brocante (antiques and junk fair) the week of August 15 at the Cour de la Mairie in the town centre. This is a good regional fair. Organised by O.G.S., 96 rue des Rosiers, Boîte Postale 73, 93400 Saint-Ouen, telephone 42.62.44.44.   Information   from   Office   de Tourisme, Jardins du Casino, 14390 Cabourg, telephone 31.91.01.09.

Caen 14000

(Please   also   see   Cabourg,   Bayeux,   and Dives-sur-Mer.)

Salon des antiquaires (antique dealers' salon) first weekend to second weekend of June, including both Saturdays and both Sundays at the Palais des Expositions. This is one of the major regional shows; you will find many Normandy antiques of all types. A fee is charged for entry. Information from M. Vermughen, C.O.M.E.T., rue Joseph-Philipport, Boîte Postale 6256, 14064 Caen Cedex, telephone 31.73.01.01.

Calais 62100

Salle des Ventes (public sales hall) auctions Sunday at 2.30 p.m. In addition to furniture, this auction offers speciality items of the region such as faïence, milk jugs, and old glass items. Four times a year, there are specialised sales of paintings, as well as jewllery and Oriental art. Inspection and buyer registration is held before the sale. Free catalogues are available upon request. Information and sales at the Salle des Ventes, 24 rue Delaroche, 62100 Calais, telephone 21.97.33.76.

Cannes 06400

Marché de la brocante (junk market) Saturday from 8 a.m. to 6 p. m. on the walks at the far end of avenue d'Antibes, which is a continuation of rue Félix Faure, the main shopping street. The market extends to the shore boulevard near the yacht harbour at allées de la Liberté opposite the old town (Suquet). The selection is best early in the morning. There are about 60 vendors, but there may be more in summer, when variety is larger, but the prices may also be higher, and there are more tourists. Information from M. Luco de Gioanni, 5 boulevard du Moulin, 06400 Cannes, telephone 93.99.22.50.

Cap d'Agde 34300

(Please see Agde.)

Castres 81100

Marché aux puces (flea market) every Saturday morning at place d'Albinque, at the beginning of the road to Albi. The market is part of the general merchandise and food market; only a couple of dozen vendors sell regional items such as pottery pitchers, folk carving, and local faience. Information from the Service du Tourisme, Théâtre Municipal, place République, 81108 Castres Cedex, telephone 63.59.92.44

Chalon-sur-Saône 71100

Petit marché aux puces (little flea market) every Friday year round at rue du Docteur-Mauchamp. This small market of not more than 20 vendors in an unremarkable town can sometimes yield interesting items such as glassware, small clay pitchers and pots, and the small silver (or more usually silver plate sometimes at solid silver prices) tastevins used for winetasting. Information from the Office de Tourisme, square Chabas, boulevard République, 71100 Chalon-sur-Saône, telephone 85.48.37.97.

Salle des Ventes (public sales hall) auction every Thursday and Saturday at 2 p.m. This market is often a good place to find massive Burgundian armoires and buffets. Buyer registration and inspection of items are held most work days and the morning of the sale. Information and sales at the Salle des Ventes, 9 rue Félix Renaud, Boîte Postale 740, 71100 Chalon-sur-Saône, telephone 85.46.39.98.

Châlons-sur-Marne 51000

Marché aux puces (flea market) last Sunday of the month year round, starting at about 7 a.m. in summer and 8 a.m. in winter at the place du Marché right in the city centre. This city, unremarkable except for the soaring cathedral (visible for miles in the open countryside), is a good source of folk art and farm furniture and especially 19th- century odds and ends. About 50 vendors attend this market, which is held indoors. Information from the Office de Tourisme, 3 quai des Arts, 51000 Châlons-sur-Marne, telephone 26.65.17.89.

Chambéry 73000

Marché à la brocante (junk market) second Saturday of every month at place Saint-Leger, a pedestrianised street in the old town centre. This market is of fair size with about 25 vendors in summer and at least 15 in winter. You'll probably see such rustic items as ox yokes, horse collars, cream pots and milk cans, but not too much furniture, crystal, jewellery, or silver. Information from the Office de Tourisme, 24 boulevard de la Colonne, 73000 Chambéry, telephone 79.33.42.47, telex 320444 F GITE SAV .

Salon des antiquaires et brocanteurs (antique and junk dealers' salon) in mid-May at the Parc des Expositions. The first two days are reserved for dealers—take your business card and a copy of your business licence. This is a large regional market; you'll find rustic furniture as well as refined items brought by some dealers from Lyon. Information from M. Jacques Allion, Foire et Salons de Savoie, Parc des Expositions, avenue du Grand Ariétaz, 73000 Chambéry, telephone 79.62.22.80.

Champagne-sur-Oise 95660

(Please also see L'Isle-Adam.)

Salon d'antiquaires et brocanteurs (antique and junk dealers' salon) the first weekend of April at the Salle des Fétes. About 70 dealers offer all types of antiques including furniture. Organised by the Groupement des Antiquaires du Vexin-Val d'Oise, 12 rue de Jaigny, 95180 Montmorency, telephone 39.60.04.56.

Charleville-Mézières 08000

Petit marché aux puces (little flea market) every Tuesday, Thursday, and Saturday at the picturesque place Ducale. This small market is part of the regular outdoor market in a relatively uninteresting town near the Belgian border. Information from the Office de Tourisme, 2 rue Mantoue, 08000 Charleville-Mézières, telephone 24.33.00.17.

Charmes 88130

La foire Vosgienne des brocanteurs (Vosges regional junk dealers' fair) last Saturday and Sunday of September at Xaronval. This is a medium-sized regional fair, where you may find old country furniture, etc. Several dozen dealers from the region sell at this fair. Information from M. Maurice LaCourt, 6 rue du Général Marion, 88130 Charmes, telephone 29.66.12.41.

Chartres 28000

Foire de la brocante (junk market) fourth Sunday and Monday of the month from May to October at the Saint Pierre church square, early morning to just after noon. This church is southeast of the cathedral down near the river. This market isn't particularly interesting, and usually has one or two dozen lacklustre sellers of small items. One shopkeeper on the square opined that Chartres is too close to Paris and too small a city to retain the best items. Free parking is available on near-by streets. Organised by the Ville de Chartres, 28019 Chartres, telephone 37.21.03.66.

Foire d'antiquaires (antique dealers' fair) last Friday to following Monday of October at the Collégiale Saint-André, just 200 metres downhill toward the river from the Cathedral. Organised by M. Ligier, Comité Saint-Pierre, 3 rue du Pont Saint-Hilaire, 28000 Chartres, telephone 37.30.90.99.

Journées brocantes et antiquités (antiques and junk days) on Acension weekend at the parc des Expositions on R.N. 10. This is a good local fair. Organised by U.C.I.A., rue de la Tonnelerie, 28000 Chartres, telephone 37.21.90.00.

Hôtel des Ventes (public sales house) auctions Tuesdays and Sundays at 2 p.m. Miscellaneous odds and ends, including jewellery, musical instruments, and old photographs and photographic equipment are sold in rapid-fire order. The inspection period is the morning before the sale. Information and sales at the Hôtel des Ven-

tes, 1 bis place Général de Gaulle, 20000
Chartres, telephone 37.36.04.33.

Chateauroux 36000

Marché aux puces (flea market) first Sunday
morning of the month from October through
June on avenue des Marins in the Quartier des
Marins, near and slightly west of the town
centre. Information from the Office de Tourisme,
place de la Gare, 36000 Chateauroux, telephone
54.34.10.74 (closed Sunday).

Salle des Ventes (public sales hall) auction every
Thursday except not in August, at 2 p.m. Inspec-
tion of merchandise and buyer registration is
held before the sale. Information and sales at the
Salle des Ventes, 5 rue Lemoine-Lenoir, 36000
Chateauroux, telephone 54.34.11.06.

Chateau-Thierry 02400

Salle des Ventes (public sales hall) auction first
and third Friday of the month at 1.45 p.m. Inspection of goods and registration is the morning
of the sale from 10 a.m. to noon. Information and
sales at the Salle des Ventes, 17bis avenue de
Soissons, 02400 Chateau-Thierry, telephone
23.83.25.05.

Chatou 78000

(Please also see Paris.)

Foire nationale à la brocante (national junk fair)
beginning of March and end of September, on the
Ile de Chatou, near Paris. This is one of the
largest antique and junk fairs in France, and is
well worth attending. Hundreds of dealers (few
private vendors) show all kinds of items. Only
truly genuine articles may be displayed and sold
at this fair. Everything from statues to crystal,
clocks, silver and silver plate, furniture, and
nearly anything else can be found at this fair.
Access from Paris by public transit to the RER

Chatou station, then walk, following signs. The five days before the official opening are reserved for the antiques trade: bring your business card and maybe a copy of a business licence or sales tax certificate with you to get in. Organised by the French antiques trade association, S. N. C. A. O. (Syndicat National du Commerce de l'Antiquité et de l'Occasion), 18 rue de Provence, 75009 Paris, telephone 47.70.88.78.

Chelles 77500

(Please also see Pontault-Combault and Paris.)

Marché aux puces (flea market) first Saturday of every month in the town centre. This is a local market, with some interesting odds and ends.

Chinon 37500

Salon des antiquaires et de la brocante (antique and junk dealers' fair) the third weekend of July in Faubourg Saint- Jacques. For information contact M. Caux, rue du 14 Faubourg Saint-Jacques, 37500 Chinon, telephoe 47.93.14.02.

Salle des Ventes (public sales hall) auction every Wednesday at 2.30 p. m. Merchandise inspection and buyer registration is held before the sale. Information and sales at the Salle des Ventes, 57 rue du Faubourg Saint-Jacques, 37500 Chinon, telephone 47.93.12.64.

Clermont-Ferrand 63000

Clermont-Ferrand, which among other claims to fame is the home of the Michelin tyre company, has several markets that move around the city and immediately adjoining suburbs. As a result, all three are listed here, out of alphabetical order. All of the markets are similar in content, since many of the sellers (both dealers and private parties) move from one to the other.

Marché aux puces (flea market) first Saturday of every month except May, August, and November and also on the third Saturday of May and November from 8 a.m. to 6 p.m. at place 1re. Mai, a large square and recreation area northeast of the city centre near the Michelin factories. Take avenue de la République to the rue de Chanteranne. You'll come to the market on the right before the end of the first block. This market offers regional furniture of Auvergne, such as rustic furniture, local faïence, jewellery, and glass, and all kinds of bric-a-brac. While only dealers are at the monthly markets on the first of the month, anyone can sell at the May and November markets. Organised by the Régies Municipales, Mairie, rue Marcombes, 63000 Clermont-Ferrand. Information from the Office de Tourisme, 69 boulevard Gergovia, 63000 Clermont-Ferrand, telephone 73.93.30.20.

Montferrand 63100

(A suburb of Clermont-Ferrand.)

Marché à la brocante (junk market) first Saturday of every month year round at place Poly, about 4 kilometres northeast of the centre of Clermont-Ferrand. This is one of the larger regional markets of central France. You're likely to see rustic faïence and domestic pottery such as wine pitchers and oil jugs. Information from the Office de Tourisme, 69 boulevard Gergovia, 63000 Clermont-Ferrand, telephone 73.93.30.20.

Royat 63130

(A suburb of Clermont-Ferrand.)

Marché aux puces et antiquités (flea and antique market) third Saturday of every month from April to October on rue Nationale, right in the centre of the old part of town. About 100 vendors prevent through traffic. Speciality items include Avergnat wickerwork, baskets and furniture, old cauldrons of iron or copper, and, rarely, local faïence. This market is the most picturesque in the region, and is located in the business district of this formerly fashionable health spa and resort. Information from the Syndicat d' Initiative, place Allard, 63130 Royat, telephone 73.35.81.87.

Colmar 68000

Marché aux puces (flea market) first and third Friday of every month from 8 a.m. until 7 p.m. at place de l'Ancienne Douane in the city's central area. This market is far larger in summer when the weather is better and the tourists more plentiful than in winter. Items at this market show Alsace's mixed French and German heritage. Look for vineyard and wine trade items, faïence in multicolour on a blue ground, pottery, etc., and occasional pieces of country furniture. (Do not get this market mixed up with the regular Thursday morning market, which takes place until noon, and is one of the more colorful street and food markets in France.) Organised by the Service des Taxes, Ville de Colmar, place de la Mairie, Boîte Postale 528, 68021 Colmar Cedex, telephone 89.23.99.68.

Salon des antiquaires (antique dealers' salon) on the first or second Wednesday to following Monday of May at the Parc des Expositions. This is a good but not grand show, with about 60 vendors, all of whom are dealers. Information from the M. Busche, Société d'Exploitation du Parc des Expositions et des Sports, avenue de la Foire-aux-Vins, 68000 Colmar, telephone 89.41.60.00.

Compiégne 60200

Salon des antiquaires (antique dealers' salon) second Thursday to second Sunday of September at the Salle Saint-Nicholas on the rue du Grand-Ferre. This show, about 80 kilometres from Paris, makes a good day trip. About 30 vendors exhibit at this show. Information from the Office de Tourisme, place de l'Hôtel de Ville, Boîte Pos-

tale 106, 60321 Compiégne Cedex, telephone
44.40.01.00, telex 145923 F OTCOMP.

Crèvecoeur-le-Grand 60300

Marché aux puces (flea market) from early morn-
ing to late afternoon on the second Thursday of
August (Assumption Day) at place de l'Hotel-de-
Ville in front of the chateau in this small town
near Beauvais. This large market has taken
place for many years, and is a true celebration.
Antiques and collectables are interesting, but
there are few regional specialities. Organised by
M. Liebbe, 1 place de l'Hôtel de Ville, 60300
Crèvecoeur-le-Grand, telephone 44.46.88.45. For
information   contact   the   Mairie,   60360
Crèvecoeur-le-Grand, telephone 44.46.87.11.

Crozon 29160

Foire à la brocante (junk fair) the first week of
April in the town center. This small town has one
of the better fairs in Brittany. Organised by
Prom'Art, 11 impasse Beethoven, 35100 Rennes,
telephone 99.50.74.19.

Cusset 03300

Salon des antiquaires et de la brocante (an- tique
and junk dealers' salon) four days (including the
weekend) during the second week of July at the
Parc du Chambon. This is a large regional fair.
Information from the Comité des Fêtes, Syndicat
d'Initiative, Mairie, rue Constitution, 03300 Cusset, telephone 70.98.77.68 or 70.31.39.44.

Dax 40100

Marché à la brocante (junk market) first
Thursday of every month year round at the place
du Marché Couvert in the centre of town near
the cathedral. This small regional market is part
of the general market; a couple of dozen vendors
sell rustic items and junk. Little in the way of

silver or art objects is at this market—it is more likely you'll find practical items such as butter moulds, stoneware and pottery crocks, and old basins. Information from the Office de Tourisme, place Thiers, Boîte Postale 177, 40104 Dax Cedex, telephone 58.74.82.33.

Deauville 14800

Salle des Ventes (public sales hall) auction every Sunday from 10 a.m. until noon and from 2 to 7 p.m. Inspection of merchandise and buyer registration is held before the sale begins. Information and sales at the Salle des Ventes, 16 rue du Général Leclerc, 14800 Deauville, telephone 31.88.21.92.

Dieppe 76200

Salle des Ventes (public sales hall) auction every Saturday year round at 2 p.m. In this seaside town in Normandy, you'll often find nautical items as well as provincial furniture, domestic pottery, and glassware. Inspection of merchandise and buyer registration take place the day before and on the morning of the sale. Information and sales at the Salle des Ventes, 53 rue de la Barre, 76200 Dieppe.

Dijon 21000

Marché aux puces (flea market) Tuesday and Friday year round from early morning until just after noon on rue de Soissons and the adjoining place de la Banque. Approximately two dozen vendors offer junk, a few antiques, and, appropriate to the home city of one of Europe's oldest universities, books. The market is only a small part of one of the most exciting street markets in France, which centres on a century-old cast iron market hall reminiscent of the now-vanished Les Halles in Paris. The cast of hundreds selling food and gadgets lure thousands of customers. Public toilets for 1 franc are available at the market hall. Street parking is difficult, since the market streets are closed to cars, and most of the narrow central streets prohibit street parking. Pay parking garages are available on boulevard de la Trémouille or under the place Grangier. Information from the Office de Tourisme, 34 rue des Forges, 21000 Dijon, telephone 80.30.35.39, telex 350912 F SI DIJON.

Salon des antiquaires et de la brocante (antique and junk dealers' salon) every May (usually the third week) at the Parc des Expositions et des Congrès, in the northeast part of the city. This is one of the larger regional sales in France, with a particularly good selection of heavy provincial furniture. A small admission charge is made. Toilets are available. A large parking lot is across the boulevard de Champagne. A large flea market takes place in mid-September at the same site. Information from M. Marc Gonnet, Parc des Expositions et Congrès de Dijon, Boîte Postale 108, 21003 Dijon Cedex, telephone 80.71.44.34, telex BURDI 350690 F Abonné 214.

Salle des Ventes (public sales hall) auctions every Wednesday and six or eight times a year on Sunday at 2 p.m. Inspection of the items to be sold and bidder registration are the morning of the sale. Information from and sales conducted by M. Emmanuel Courlet de Vregille, Salle des Ventes, 44 rue de Gray (near the place du 30 Octobre on the east side of town), 21000 Dijon, telephone 80.73.17.64.

Salle des Ventes (public sales hall) auctions every Thursday at 9.30 a.m. and 2 p.m. Inspection and bidder registration is held the day before and the morning of the sale. Information from and sales conducted by M. Philippe Sadde, Salle des Ventes, 13 rue Paul Cabet, 21000 Dijon, telephone 80.66.19.17.

Salle des Ventes (public sales hall) auctions every Friday at 2 p.m. Inspection and bidder registration is the morning of the sale. Information from and sales conducted by M. Levitte, 45 rue des Godrans, 21000 Dijon, telephone 80.30.59.41.

Dives-sur-Mer 14160

Marché aux puces (flea market) last Sunday of
the month year round beginning about 8 a.m. on
at the town market hall just north the rue Gaston Manneville (the road to Lisieux) at the
church. There are far fewer tourists in winter
than in summer, since this town is adjacent to
the summer beach resort of Cabourg. Information from the Office de Tourisme, Jardins de
Casino, 14390 Cabourg, telephone 31.91.01.09

Divonne-les-Bains 01220

Grande foire aux antiquaires et brocanteurs (antique and junk dealers' fair) third weekend of
August all day at the place du Marché in the
centre of this exquisite resort overlooking Lake
Geneva (Lac Léman). Information from the Office de Tourisme, rue des Bains, 01220 Divonne-
les-Bains, telephone 50.20.01.22.

Salon des antiquaires de Divonne-les-Bains (antique dealers' salon) third weekend of May. This
is a relatively new fair. Organised by Prom'Art,
11 impasse Beethoven, 35100 Rennes, telephone
99.50.74.19.

Douai 59500

(Please also see Lille.)

Braderie brocante (junk festival) first Sunday of
October in the city centre. This is also a tradi-
tional folk festival. Organised by the Union des
Commerçants, Boîte Postale 235, 59500 Douai
Cedex, telephone 27.88.93.76.

Dourdan

(Please also see Etampes.)

Foire de la brocante (junk fair) second weekend
of December in this small town southwest of
Paris. About 35 vendors sell all types of antiques

and collectables. Copies and reworked or trans-
formed items are prohibited at this fair. Organised by the Association de Brocanteurs de
Seine-et-Marne (A.B.S.E.M.), 100 rue de Général
de Gaulle, 77780 Bourron-Marlotte, telephone
60.70.14.95.

Draguignan 83300

(Please also see Fayence and Flayosc.)

Salon d'antiquités et brocante du Var (antique
and junk salon of Var) the first weekend of
February at the Maison des Sports. About 130
exhibitors show all types of antiques and junk.
Parking is available at the show venue. Or-
ganised by M. Michel Allongue, 9 Quartier de la
Tourettes, 83440 Fayence, telephone 94.76.11.11
or 94.76.17.92. Information from the Office de
Tourisme, 9 boulevard Clemenceau, 83300
Draguignan, telephone 94.68.63.30.

Duclair 76480

Salle des Ventes (public sales hall) auctions
every Sunday at 2 p.m. Inspection and buyer
registration is held in the morning and just
before the sale begins. Sales and information
from Salle des Ventes, 129 rue Jules Ferry, 76480
Duclair, telephone 35.37.50.61.

Durtal 49430

(Please also see Angers.)

Grande rendez-vous de la brocante (grand junk
meet) last Sunday of September all day (beginning early, about 5:30 a.m.) in this town near
Angers. This is one of the largest once-a-year
markets in France, with over five hundred vendors mainly from surrounding regions, but some
from elsewhere. Many small items—including
faience and pottery, vineyard equipment and old
bottles, as well as 19th-century furniture and old
gas lamps and chandeliers. Occasionally you'll

find silver and arms. Information is available from the organisers, Association Angevine Arts et Traditions Populaires (A.A.A.T.P.), Mme. Bellec, La Jocolière, 123 Grand' Rue, 4914 Jarzé, telephone 41.89.42.65, or M. Marc Roy, 5 rue Geoffroy l'Asnier, 75004 Paris, telephone 42.77.83.44.

Eauze 32800

Salon des antiquaires (antique dealers' salon) for one week and two weekends during the first half of May. (Even after 16 years, they haven't got the dates consistent for every year!) The entire village centre serves as the market place. Information from M. Fourtou, Syndicat d'Initiative, place Mairie, 32800 Eauze, telephone 62.09.85.62.

Enghien-les-Bains 95880

Salle des Ventes (public sales hall) auctions usually twice a month (call for exact dates and times). This suburban town is only about 12 kilometres from Paris, and the items offered reflect Parisian tastes and prices. You'll especially find modern paintings and 19th-century furniture. Information and sales at the Salle des Ventes, 2 rue du Docteur Leray, 95880 Enghien-les-Bains, telephone (1) 34.12.68.16, fax (1) 34.12.89.64.

Foire d'antiquités et brocante (antique and junk fair) in mid January at the Salle des Fêtes. This is a reasonably large fair, which benefits in quality but not price from its proximity to Paris. Information from Groupement des Antiquaires du Vexin-Val d'Oise, 12 rue de Jaigny, 95160 Montmorency, telephone (1) 39.60.04.56.

Epinal 88000

(Please also see Charmes.)

Foire de printemps de l'antiquité (spring antiques fair) Easter weekend (Good Friday

through Easter Monday) at the Parc des Expositions. This is a large and well-reputed regional
fair. For information, contact M. Andre Viant,
Syndicat des Antiquaires et Brocanteurs de Vosges, 47 route de Remiremont, 88000 Epinal,
telehone 29.35.34.85.

Etampes 91150

Salon des antiquaires (antique dealers' salon) Ascension weekend (usually in May) from Thursday
to Sunday from 10 a.m. to 7 p.m. at the Salle des
Fêtes, Parc des Expositions, on avenue Bon-
nevaux. The Wednesday before the show opens to
the public is reserved for members of the antiques trade; bring a business card and maybe a
copy of a business licence. This is a regional show
with about 35 exhibitors, sponsored by the local
Lions Club. There is regional rustic furniture
(some meant only for very high ceilings), faïence,
even old plumbing fixtures. Information from M.
Jean-Pierre Locquet, La Libéronière, 815 rue
Juliot Curie, 91150 Saclas, telephone (1)
64.95.62.18, telex 604541 F, fax (1) 60.80.96.85.

Ferté-Alais 77700

(Please also see Etampes.)

Foire de brocante (junk fair) first weekend of
November in this small village east of Paris.
About 35 vendors offer all types of used items
and antiques, including some furniture, jewellery, and glass. Reproductions are prohibited at
this fair. Organised by the Association de Brocanteurs de Seine- et-Marne (A.B.S.E.M.), 100 rue
du Géneéral de Gaulle, 77780 Bourron-Marlotte,
telephone 60.70.14.95.

Fayence 83440

Foire de antiquité et de la brocante (antique and
junk fair) Ascension weekend (beginning of May),
first weekend of August, and the All Saint's
weekend at place de l'Eglise in the centre of this

Provençal village. About 80 vendors offer provençl furniture and small items. Information from M. Michel Allongue, Quartier du Lac-de-Tourettes, 83440 Fayence, telephone 94.76.11.11 or 94.76.17.92.

Flayosc 83780

(Please also see Fayence and Draguignan.)

Marché à la brocante (junk market) last Sunday of every month in the centre of this small town in the hills of Provence near Draguignan. This is a relatively small but refreshing market, where you may see rustic Provençal items such as painted glassware, winegrowers' items, and occasional pieces of folk art.

The whole village centre turns into a market from the end of June to the third week of July. Information from the Office de Tourisme, boulevard Général de Gaulle, 83700 Flayosc, telephone 94.40.41.31.

Fontainebleau 77300

Salle des Ventes (public sales hall) auction every Friday and Sunday afternoon. The items here run more toward high finish and elegance than country rusticity. You may find bronze statues, cut-glass chandeliers, and beautiful furniture of oak or fruitwood. Inspection of merchandise and buyer registration is held Wednesday sales and in the morning before the weekend sales. Information and sales at the Salle des Ventes, 5 rue Royale, place du Château, 77300 Fontainebleau, telephone (1) 64.22.27.62.

Journées nationales de brocante (national junk days) in mid-April (usually third weekend but can vary) near the chateau. This is a good regional sale, with about 100 vendors. Reproductions and altered works are prohibited. Organised by the Association de Brocanteurs de Seine-et-Marne (A.B.S.E.M.), 100 rue du Géneéral de Gaulle, 77780 Bourron-Marlotte, telephone 60.70.14.95.

Biennale de Fontainebleau (Fontainebleau biennial) at the end of April and beginning of May near the Chateau. This is a good regional show. Organised by SADEMA, 47 boulevard Blanqui, 75013 Paris, telephone (1) 45.65.95.95.

Gien 45500

Foire des antiquités et brocante (antique and junk fair) the fourth weekend (Saturday, Sunday, and Monday) of August on the Esplanade de la Loire and Quai de Sully. This lively sale on the south bank of the Loire (across the bridge from the main part of Gien) draws about 100 vendors, with lots of items, including old harnesses and tack, hunting items, provincial furniture, and chandeliers. Many but not all vendors are dealers, mainly from the region. Information is available from M. Germain, A.C.A. de Gien, Mairie de Gien, 45500 Gien, telephone 38.67.00.01.

Granville 50400

Salle des Ventes (public sales hall) auction every Saturday or Sunday year round at 2.30 p.m. Inspection and buyer registration is held before the auction begins. This market has specialities of the region, including faïence, domestic pottery, copper pots and pans, and, occasionally, heavy provincial furniture, especially armoires (often more than 8 feet tall). Information and sales at the Salle des Ventes, rue Jeanne Jugan, 50499 Granville, telephone 33.50.03.01.

Givors 69700

(Please also see Lyon.)

Marché aux puces (flea market) the third Saturday of every month in the town centre. This is a good suburban market, and has all other types of goods and food in addition to antiques and junk.

Foire à a la paperasserie (paper and print fair) second weekend of November at the Palais des Sports. This is a large local specialists' fair. Information from M.J.C., 1 rue des Tuileries, 69700 Givors, telephone 78.73.09.02.

Grenoble 38000

Marché à la brocante (junk market) third Monday of the month year round at place Saint-André in the old city centre. This market seems to be where dealers buy and sell among themselves. Finds of regional items can be made here, but there's not much furniture. Information from the Office de Tourisme, 14 rue de la République, Boîte Postale 227, 380019 Grenoble Cedex, telephone 76.54.34.36.

Marché aux puces (flea market) every Sunday from 8 a.m. to 1 p.m. on rue de Stalingrad in the car park of the "Super Pakbo" supermarket. This is a new market, and attracts local residents as vendors as well as potential buyers. For information, contact the Office de Tourisme, or the organiser at 76.87.89.28.

Marché aux puces du vieux Grenoble (flea market of old Grenoble) second Sunday of the month from March to June and October to December on rue Saint-Laurent, only a short way from the river Isère in the old city centre. The setting is picturesque, in one of the major provincial cities of France. Likely finds include cream pots and water jugs, butter molds, and occasional religious items. Information from the Office de Tourisme, 14 rue de la République, Boîte Postale 227, 380019 Grenoble, telephone 76.54.34.36.

Salon Européen des antiquaires (European antique dealers' salon) every year for 10 days around the end of January and first week of February at the Alpexpo congress hall, about 5 kilometres south of the town centre on avenue J. Perrot near the Village Olympique.

Information from Mme. Verdelhan, Alpexpo,
Palais des Expositions, Avenue d'Innsbrück,
Boîte Postale 788, 38029 Grenoble Cedex,
telephone 76.09.80.26, or at the Alpexpo grounds,
76.39.66.00.

Guingamp 22200

Foire à la brocante (junk fair) fourth weekend
(including Friday) of October at the Hall des
Foires et Expositions in this small Breton town.
This is a minor regional fair. Information from
Foire Exposition de Guingamp, Boîte Postale
171, 22204 Guingamp Cedex, telephone
96.43.75.99.

Havre

(Please see Le Havre.)

Hericourt 70400

Marché aux puces (flea market) third Sunday of
every month year round. This relatively small
market is of slight interest, though you may find
old copper casseroles and faïence.

Hyères 83400

Marché aux puces (flea market) every Sunday
morning on avenue de la Pinade in the La Capte
district. This lively market in a Mediterranean
shore town near Toulon is part of the colourful
food and general merchandise market. Vendors
offer glassware (but not crystal), maritime items,
souvenirs, some folk art, and a few wood carvings. Information from Mairie de la Capte, 83400
Hyères, telephone 94.58.00.45.

Isle-Adam

(Please see L'Isle-Adam.)

Isle-sur-Sorgue

(Please see L'Isle-sur-Sorgue.)

Joigny 89300

Salle des Ventes (public sales hall) auction every Saturday or Sunday (it varies) at 2:30 p.m. This picturesque Burgundian town is often a good source of 19th-century furniture and occasional old tapestries. Inspection of merchandise and buyer registration is held the the day before and morning of the sale. Information and sales at the Salle des Ventes, 34 rue Aristide Briand, 89300 Joigny, telephone 86.62.00.75.

Joyeuse 07260

Foire à la brocante (junk fair) the weekend following August 15 in the village centre. This relatively small market has been held regularly over the years. For information contact the Comité des Fétes, Mairie de Joyeuse, 07260 Joyeuse, telephone 75.39.40.19.

Lacroix-Saint-Ouen 60610

Hôtel des Ventes des Particuliers (public sales hall) auctions irregularly during the year. Only furniture and wood items are dealt with at this auction. Information and sales conducted by Service Conseil des Frères Nordin at the Hôtel des Ventes, 4 bis avenue de la Forêt, 60610 Lacroix-Saint-Ouen, telephone 44.41.56.88.

Lamorlaye 60260

Exposition d'antiquaires (antique dealers' exposition) at the beginning of October at the Salle des Fêtes. This is a minor show with several dozen dealers, held in this town not too far from Paris. Information from Groupement des Antiquaires du Vexin-Val-d'Oise, 12 rue de Jaigny, 95160 Montmorency, telephone 30.60.04.56.

Laon 02000

Salles des Ventes (public sales hall) auction every Saturday at 2:30 p.m. year round. Inspection and buyer registration take place before the sale begins. Information and sales at Salles des Ventes, 1 rue Roze, 02000 Laon, telephone 23.23.47.27.

La Rochelle 17000

Marché aux puces (flea market) every Saturday from April to September and the first and third Saturday of months from October to March on rue St. Nicolas. This is part of the regular food and fish market; the setting is picturesque and often more interesting than the items and collectables offered. There is normal bric-a-brac, massive copper basins, and occasionally odds and ends from Asia and the Caribbean. At one time, La Rochelle was the main seaport of France, with a monopoly over trade with France's colonies. Information from the Office de Tourisme, 10 rue Fleuriau, 17000 La Rochelle, telephone 46.41.14.68.

La Seyne-sur-Mer 83500

Marché à la brocante (junk market) first and third Wednesday and Sunday except July of every month at place de la Lune. This market is a typical colourful Provençal market, with both tourist souvenirs and assorted normal flea market items. Information from the Office de Tourisme, place Ledru Rollin, 83500 La Seyne-sur-Mer, telephone 94.94.73.09. Organised by the Hôtel de Ville, quai Saturnin Fabri, 83500 La Seyne-sur-Mer, telephone 94.06.95.00.

Le Luc 83340

Marché à la brocante (junk market) every Saturday morning at Aux Liébords. This market in Provence has some interesting items such as glass (not crystal) and, sometimes, folk art. Information from the Office de Tourisme, Place Verdun, 83340 Le Luc, telephone 94.60.74.51 (open only from June 1 to August 31),

Le Mans 72000

Marché aux puces (flea market) every Friday morning on avenue de Paderborn at the foot of the cathedral, along the tree-shaded gardens. Information from the Office de Tourisme, Hôtel des Ursulines, rue de l'Etoile, 72000 Le Mans, telephone 43.28.17.22, telex 720006 F.

24 heures de la brocante (24 hours of junk) usually the second weekend of April (including Friday) throughout the old town above the river and near the cathedral. This is a major regional fair and worth the visit. Information from Prom'Art, 11 impasse Beethoven, 35000 Rennes, telephone 99.50.74.19.

Salon d'antiquaires (antique dealers' salon) the first week of December (exact dates vary from year to year) at the Abbaye de l'Epau, about 4 kilometres southeast of the city centre on D152. This salon is in the exquisite setting of an ancient abbey. Organised by Promex, Boòte Postale 232, 61007 Alençon, telephone 33.29.31.10.

Le Puy 43000

Petit marché aux puces (small flea market) Saturday morning from just before 8 a.m. to noon, at the place de Clauzel as part of the regular food market. There are usually only about a dozen vendors of antiques and junk. Le Puy is in a relatively poor part of France, but is one of the most beautiful of French towns in part because of the spiny heights that tower several hundred feet above the surrounding plains. Information from the Office de Tourisme, place du Breuil (only a couple of hundred metres from the market), 43000 Le Puy, telephone 71.09.27.42.

Les Sables d'Olonne 85100

Marché aux puces (flea market) first Sunday of
the month year round at place de la Chaume.
This Atlantic seaside summer resort's market is
nothing special; you may find vendors offering
marine items, local pottery, and small agricultural tools. Information from the Office de
Tourisme, rue Maréchal Leclerc, 85100 Les
Sables d'Olonne, telephone 51.32.03.28.

Lille 59000

Lille and its surrounding area are hardly tourist
country: full of slag heaps, grimy brick buildings,
and steel mills. However, it is full of promise for
the antique collector and dealer, because it is the
centre of France's decaying and economically
depressed Rust Belt.

(Please also see Douai and Roubaix.)

Marché de Wazemmes (Wazemmes market) Sunday morning year round from dawn to about
noon around the Parvis de Croix and place de la
Nouvelle Aventure and surrounding the Eglise
Saint-Pierre (church). The general market, with
food, clothes, and miscellaneous items, occupies a
paved space and a 19th-century cast-iron market
hall, but the flea market is off to the east side.
About 120 dealers and private parties sell all
kinds of items, including silver and silver plate,
brass, crystal chandeliers, bottles and glass, old
signs, and lots of 19th-century furniture, including chairs, chests of drawers, and hope chests.
This is one of the best flea markets in France:
prices are reasonable and quality is relatively
high.
    Parking is available on the street, but is
difficult to find after 8 a.m. Access by public
transport to the Gambetta station, then walk to
the church, visible over one row of houses.
Information from the Office de Tourisme, Palais
Rihour, place Rihour, 59000 Lille, telephone
20.30.81.00, telex 110213 F TOURLIL. A branch
tourist office is found at the main railway
station.

Grande braderie (grand braderie) the first Monday after the first Sunday of September in the Vielle Ville (old town centre). This is a large fair, with hundreds of vendors offering all types of used items and antiques. Organised by the city. Parking is difficult to impossible near the fair, though street parking is found in the deserted streets a ways from from the festivities. Access by public transport to the Rihour station, which is in the city centre. Information from the Office de Tourisme, Palais Rihour, place Rihour, 59000 Lille, telephone 20.30.81.00, telex 110213 F TOURLIL.

Salon de l'antiquité et de la brocante (antique and junk biennial show) second weekend of October every year at the Foire Internationale de Lille, near the main railway station. This is one of the major provincial shows in France, and is well worth attending. Access by car is from the avenue Julien Destrée exit from the ring road. The nearest subway station is Gares, at the railway station; then walk several hundred metres. Organised by M. Gauthier, Norexpo, Boîte 523, 59022 Lille Cedex, telephone 20.52.79.60.

Salle des Ventes (public sales hall) auctions every Saturday at 2 p.m. Inspection and registration take place Friday from 2 to 6 p.m. and Saturday morning from 9 to 12 a.m. Information and sales at the Salle de Ventes, 14 rue des Jardins, 59000 Lille, telephone 20.06.10.14.

Salle des Ventes (public sales hall) auctions every Monday at 2 p.m. Inspection and bidder registration takes place Saturday from 9 to 12 a.m. and Monday from 9 to 11 a.m. Information and sales at the Salle des Ventes, 2 rue Sainte-Anne, 59000 Lille, telephone 20.06.25.81.

Limoges 87000

Petit marché aux puces (little flea market) every Wednesday and Saturday from early morning until about 12:30 p.m. at the tree-shaded place d'Aine (facing the Palais de Justice), a short distance from the food and general market. You'll often find minor pieces of Limoges porcelain, but most will be of medium to low quality. You also may find farm implements, andirons, pokers, and shovels. Information from the Office de Tourisme, boulevard de Fleurus, 87000 Limoges, telephone 55.34.46.87, telex 580705 F.

Marché aux puces (flea market) last Sunday of every month on rue Brousseau in the city centre. All types of items can be found at this markets. Information from the Office de Tourisme, boulevard de Fleurus, 87000 Limoges, telephone 55.34.46.87, telex 580705 F.

L'Isle-Adam 95290

Petit marché aux puces (little flea market) third Sunday of every month in this small town in Paris' outskirts. Because of its proximity to Paris, prices are as high as in Paris and selection is similar though much smaller. Information from the Office de Tourisme, 1 avenue de Paris, 95290 L'Isle-Adam, telephone 34.69.09.76.

L'Isle-sur-la-Sorgue 84800

This small town in Provence, near Avignon and Cavaillon, promotes itself as an antiques centre. There are frequent large markets and fairs, some of the best in the region.

Marché aux puces et isle de la brocante (flea market and junk island), two markets that face each other across the water in the village centre. The junk market takes place all day Saturday and Sunday, and can attract over 100 vendors on some days. The flea market, also on the water, takes place all day Sunday, though it quietens down around lunch time. These markets are often places to find Provençal antiques, such as carved olive wood, pottery, glassware, and, rarely, Santons dolls. Information from M. Albert Gassier, O.R.S.E.F., Boîte Postale 45, 84800 L'-Isle-sur-la-Sorgue, telephone 90.38.10.43.

Foire à la brocante (junk fair) three times a year: Easter Week and the Easter Monday (the day after Easter), Pentecost (in May), and the Assumption Day weekend (second Thursday to the following Monday of August). This fair is a much larger version of the regular markets and, especially in August, attracts thousands of visitors. Information from M. Albert Gassier, O.R.S.E.F., Boîte Postale 45, 84800 L'Isle-sur-la-Sorgue, telephone 90.38.10.43.

Village d'antiquaires et brocanteurs (antique and junk dealers' village) open Saturday, Sunday, and Monday year round at Village d'Antiquaires et Brocanteurs next to the railway station. This building is home to about 40 dealers, who offer large quantities of Provençal furniture, folk items such as glassware, farm tools, and copper cauldrons, and just plain junk, but no readily apparent reproductions. For information call 90.38.17.44.

Liseaux 14100

(Please also see Bernay.)

Salon de l'objet ancien et multi-collections (salon of antique object and collections) the end of April and beginning of May at the Parc des Expositions. Information from Mme. Dufiel, 34 rue de Bras, 14000 Caen, telephone 31.86.43.38.

Lyon 69000

The ancient city of Lyon dates from before the days of the Romans; Roman ruins can be seen. For centuries Lyon has been rich: a major crossroads and centre of the cloth trade, and an early centre of printing. It is also widely acknowledged to be the home of the best of French cuisine.

Marché aux puces de la Feyssine (flea market at Feyssine) Saturday and especially Sunday morning year round from early morning (6 a.m. for members of the antiques trade and 7 a.m. for the

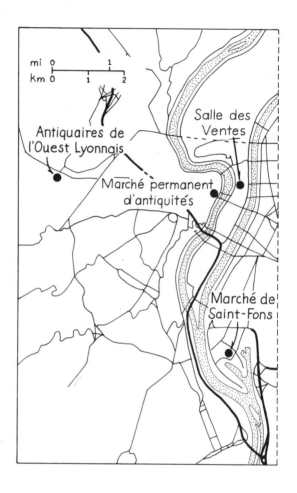

mi 0   1
Km 0   1   2

Antiquaires de
l'Ouest Lyonnais

Salle des
Ventes

Marché permanent
d'antiquités

Marché de
Saint-Fons

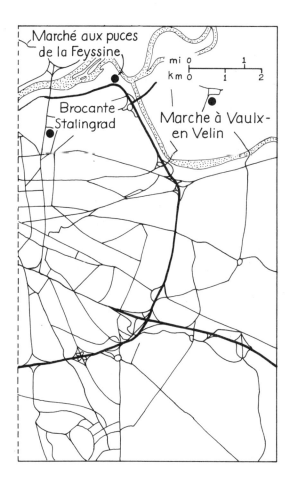

Marché aux puces
de la Feyssine

Brocante
Stalingrad

Marche à Vaulx-
en Velin

mi 0   1
km 0   1   2

public) to about 1 p.m. at in the northeastern suburb of Villeurbanne, upstream along the Rhone canal. This grubby market is by far the largest in Lyon. Hundreds of (mostly Arab) vendors push piles of used clothing, car parts, bike parts, and used cars as you approach the octagonal building in the centre of the large dusty (or muddy) field.

The building in the centre is where about 200 dealers offer a jumble of small antiques and lots of junk in the permanent stalls and tables rented by the day in the octagon's open-air centre. While there are thousands of items, including glass, silver, porcelain, massive furniture, and ironwork, this is one market where you need to know exactly what you're looking at. There are no warranties or guarantees given at this market. Toilets are available in the building, are filthy, and cost 1 franc.

Parking is difficult and frustrating; only distant street parking is available, since only sellers can park on the grounds. Park where you can and follow the crowds. Access by public transport on the Metro to the Bonnevay station, then walk along the canal, and cross the first bridge you come to, following the crowds, or take buses 51, 56, or 57 to the corner of the Pont de Plaisance and rue Balland, and then walk. Information from M. Lucien Monier, Amicale des Brocanteurs de Feyssine-le-Haut, 17-19 rue Rouget-de-l'Isle, 69100 Villeurbanne, telephone 78.93.40.19 for information or 78.93.44.37 for the market commissioner.

Marché aux puces de Vaulx-en-Velin (flea market in Vaulx-en-Valin) all day Saturday and every Sunday morning from 7 a.m. until noon in rue Tita Coïs in the centre of this suburb northeast of the Lyon city centre. This market is part of a large street market with over 500 vendors near the centre of this suburb northeast of Lyon. It is in the same general direction as the market in Feyssine but across the canal; a visit to both is possible. Access is from the autoroute junction Vaulx-en-Velin-centre. Parking is difficult. For information, call 78.80.96.55.

Marché aux puces de Saint-Fons every Sunday morning from 7 a.m. to noon at Port Edouard Herriot at 1 boulevard Sampaix, south of the city centre on the east bank of the Rhône. All kinds of items can be found at this market, but it is smaller than the two above. Organised by the Mairie de Saint-Fons, telephone 78.70.94.70.

Brocante Stalingrad (Stalingrad junk market) Thursday and Saturday from about 8:30 a.m. until noon and 2 p.m. to 6 p.m., and Sunday from 9 a.m. to 1 p.m. at 115 Boulevard Stalingrad, across the railway tracks from the Parc de la Tête d'Or. The name "brocante" belies the place: in actuality it is an antique dealers' centre, containing approximately 150 dealers of medium to high quality items. A few items are of museum quality (and priced accordingly, though less than usual in Paris). You'll find massive furniture from the 17th to early 20th centuries, porcelain and crystal in abundance, massive silver flatware and quantities of silver plate, paintings (mainly from the 19th century), bronzes, and a few old books. These items are often refined rather than country-style primitives. Thursdays are peaceful; this is the day the antique trade comes. Weekends are crowded, boisterous, and it takes far longer to see what there is.

Parking is easy on Thursday on Boulevard Stalingrad directly across from the market between the street and the railroad embankment. On weekends, either arrive very early or plan to walk quite a way. Access by Metro to the Brotteaux station, then follow the tracks north for about 500 metres. Information from Brocante Stalingrad, 115 boulevard Stalingrad, 69100 Villeurbanne, telephone 78.89.30.68 or 78.93.91.25.

Marché permanent d'antiquités (permanent antique dealers' market) open weekdays from about 9 to 12 a.m. and 3 to 6 p.m. on Quai Romain-Rolland along the west bank of the Saône river in the old medieval section of Lyon. Several dozen dealers offer good-quality items at relatively high prices. Access by Metro to the Cordeliers station, then 300 walk metres west and across the river to the Quai Romain-Rolland. Parking is available in car parks between the Quai and the river, though on weekdays these are often crowded. Street parking is hard to find.

Les Antiquaires de l'Ouest Lyonnais (antique dealers of west Lyon) open weekdays from 10 to 12 a.m. and 2 to 7 p.m. on ave 13-15 avenue E. Millau in the western suburb of Craponne. Two dozen dealers have permanent installations in this antiques market. Access by car on D11 to Craponne. Information from les Antiquaires de l'Ouest Lyonnais, Grande Route de Craponne, 13/15 avenue E. Millau, 69200 Craponne, telephone 78.44.61.77.

Foire de Brocante (junk fair) the middle of May and October on quai Achille Lignon. For exact details, contact M. Pierre Thoral, 15 rue Chinard, 69009 Lyon, telephone 78.83.81.63.

Salle des Ventes (public sales hall) auction every Monday and Wednesday at 2 p.m. Viewing and buyer registration is accomplished in the morning before the sale from 9 to 11 a.m. Information and sales at the Salle des Ventes, 31 rue des Tuiliers, 69008 Lyon, telephone 78.00.86.65.

Nouvel Hôtel des Ventes (new public sales hall) auctions twice a week, usually at 2 p.m. Viewing and buyer registration is before the sale. Information and sales at the Nouvel Hôtel des Ventes, 3 rue de Cronstadt, 69007, telephone 72.73.45.67.

Ventes aux Encheres par les Douanes (Customs auctions) at irregular intervals. All types of unclaimed goods, goods where customs formalities have not been met, and other miscellaneous goods are offered. Information and sales at the Ventes aux Encheres par les Douanes, 6 rue Charles Bienner, 69002 Lyon, telephone 78.42.17.17.

Hôtel des Ventes (public sales hall) has auctions at irregular intervals. Viewing and registration is before the sale. Information and sales at the Hôtel des Ventes, 3 avenue Sidoine Appolinaire, 69009 Lyon, telephone 78.47.78.18.

Mâcon 71000

Salle des Ventes (public sales hall) auction every
Saturday at 2.30 p.m. You're likely to find fine
old walnut Burgundian furniture and chairs at
this sale. Buyer registration and inspection of
merchandise takes place the day before and on
the morning of the sale. Information and sales at
the Salle des Ventes, 1054 Quai de Lattre-de-Tassigny, 71000 Mâcon, telephone 85.38.75.07.

Foire à la brocante (junk fair) the first weekend
of December at the Palais de la Foire along the
river on the north side of the town. This is a
relatively small regional fair. Information from
Promonet, 401 rue de Fontenailles, 71000
Mâcon.

Magny-en-Vexin 95000

Salon d'antiquités et brocante (antique and junk
salon) in mid-June (exact dates vary from year to
year) at the Salle des Fêtes. This is a small fair
not too far from Paris. Information from Groupement des Antiquaires du Vexin-Val'd'Oise, 12 rue
de Jaigny, 95160 Montmorency, telephone
39.60.04.56.

Maisons-Laffitte 78600

Exposition d'antiquaires (antique show) at the
Chateau in September (contact the organiser for
exact dates). Organised by the Groupement des
Antiquaires du Vexin-Val'd'Oise, 12 rue de Jaigny, 95160 Montmorency, telephone 39.60.04.56.

Marseille 13000

(Please also see Aubagne.)

Hôtel des Ventes du Prado (Prado public sales
hall) auctions every Wednesday, Friday, and
Saturday at 2.30 p.m. at 19 rue Borde. Public
inspection and registration is held before the
sale. Information from the Hôtel Ventes du

Prado, 19 rue Borde, 13008 Marseille, telephone 91.79.46.30.

Salon des antiquaires (antique dealers' salon) third week of October from 10 a.m. to 7 p.m. at the Parc Chanot convention hall on the southern side of Marseille along boulevards Rabatau and Michelet. This is one of the major regional shows in southern France, with an emphasis on jewellery. The fair is open to members of the antiques trade for two days before the public is admitted. Bring a copy of your business licence or business card. Organised by M. Grobon Ghiglione, S.A. Foire International de Marseille, Parc Chanot, Bôite Postale 2, 13266 Marseille Cedex 8, telephone 91.76.16.00, telex 410021 F.

Quartier de cours Julien (Julien Court arcade) antique row, a tree-shaded street home to about 30 permanent dealers. The second Sunday of the month, the shops spill out into the street, especially in the morning. This street is just off the cours Lieutand not far from La Canebière, the colourful boulevard that is the heart of Marseille. Information from cours Julien, telephone 91.42.79.35.

Mauvezin 32120

Foire à la brocante (junk fair) at the beginning of April (exact dates vary from year to year) in the centre of this small town west of Toulouse. This is mainly a local affair. For information contact G.I.A.R., avenue Jean Baylet, 31000 Toulouse.

Meaux 77100

Marché aux puces (flea market) last Sunday of every month in the town centre. This is not a major market, since it is too close to Paris (about 50 kilometres). Information from the Office de Tourisme, 2 rue Notre-Dame, 77100 Meaux, telephone 64.33.02.26.

Salle des Ventes (public sales hall) auction every Saturday and some Sundays at 2 p.m. The proximity to Paris tends to bring out more highly polished items than country pieces. You'll find furniture, crystal, some porcelains, mostly from the 19th century. Inspection of items and buyer registration is held in the morning before the sale. Information and sales at the Salle des Ventes, 54 rue de l'Abreuvoir, 77100 Meaux, telephone 64.34.11.97.

Menton 06500

Marché à la brocante (junk market) every Friday year round as part of the public market on place aux Herbes. Parking is available in a lot across the street. This small market draws fewer tourists than those of Nice or Cannes. Information from the Office de Tourisme, at the Palais de l'Europe on avenue Boyer, Boîte Postale 111, 06503 Menton Cedex, telephone 93.57.57.00, telex 462207 F OFFTOUR.

Méounes 83136

Marché aux puces (flea market) the first Saturday of the month, (including a general market) and marché à la brocante (junk market) every Monday morning (early!) at the cour de la Mairie. In addition, there are large four-day marchés a à la brocante 11 to 14 July, and around Assumption Day (August 15). These markets in this village near Toulon in Mediterranean Provence are well worth a visit to find rustic junk, including rustic glass, small pieces of furniture, minor jewellery, as well as normal bric-a-brac and bibelots. For information, contact M. R. Niccoletti, La Demeurence, 83136 Méounes, telephone 94.33.94.54.

Metz 57000

Marché aux puces (flea market) first and third Saturday of every month year round from 7 a.m. to noon at the grounds of the Foire Internationale in the suburban Grigy district. Here you'll find about 200 vendors in Halls 1, 3, 4, and 5;

among the junk you may find furniture, clocks, paintings, crystal (especially Saint-Louis, which is manufactured near Metz), jewellery and silverware, books, postcards, faïence, and heavy copperware. Only used goods may be sold, but Nazi relics are forbidden. Parking is available at the venue, which is 5 kilometres southeast of the Metz city centre on D955. Access by bus is on special line ("Service Special Marché aux Puces") every 45 minutes from 6.30 a.m. until noon. The bus stops at place de la Republique, the railway station, Lacretelle, and the cemetery. Organised by the Foire Internationale de Metz, Parc des Expositions, Boîte Postale 5059, 57072 Metz Cedex 3, telephone 87.75.49.55, telex 930196 F FIMETZ. Information also from the Office de Tourisme, place d'Armes, 57000 Metz, telephone 87.75.65.21, fax 87.l36.59.43, telex 860411 F.

Marché aux puces (flea market) second and fourth Saturday of every month at the place de la Nation in the suburb of Montigny-les-Metz. This is a smaller market than the one held at the fairgrounds, but many of the same vendors participate in both. Access by car on from N57 south from the Metz city centre. Parking can be difficult. Information from the Office de Tourisme, place d'Armes, 57000 Metz, telephone 87.75.65.21, telex 860411 F.

Foire des brocanteurs (junk dealers' fair) second Sunday of September from 10 a.m. to 7 p.m. throughout the old Quartier Outre Seille in the city centre. All types of junk and used items are offered for sale. Organised by the Association des Artisans, Commerçants, et Professions Libérales d'Outre Seille. Information from the Office de Tourisme, place d'Armes, 57000 Metz, telephone 87.75.65.21, telex 860411 F.

Marché aux puces de Noël (Christmas flea market) the first Sunday of December from 9 a.m. to 6 p.m. throughout the city centre. In addition to antiques and junk, toys and some new items are also sold. Information from the Office de Tourisme, place d'Armes, 57000 Metz, telephone 87.75.65.21, telex 860411 F.

Salon des antiquaires (antique dealers' salon) Friday to Monday in the second half of November. You may find beautiful rustic pine furniture and exquisite fruitwood marquetry furniture at this fair, as well as quantities of crystal, silver, jewellery, tapestries, paintings, prints, etchings, and silver plate. This is a major regional fair, and is well worth attending. Organised by M. Vayssade, Salon des Antiquaires, Foire Internationale de Metz, Boîte Postale 5059, 57072 Metz Cedex 3, telephone 87.75.49.55, telex 930196 F FIMETZ.

Meyrargues 13650

Foire des brocanteurs (junk dealers' fair) the end of May and beginning of June (varies from year to year) throughout this small town. This major regional fair, near Aix-en-Provence, has almost 150 vendors (mostly dealers) with all kinds of bibelots, folk art, faience, and other odds and ends. Information from the organiser, M. Claude Giraud, 1 rue Frédéric Mistral, 13650 Meyrargues, telephone 42.57.50.57.

Milly-le-Forêt 91490

(Please also see Ferté-Alais, Etampes, Fontainebleau, and Moret-sur-Loing.)

Foire à la brocante (junk fair) second weekend of March in the village centre. This is a good regional fair, with about 30 vendors of furniture, small items, and collectables. Reproductions are prohibited at this fair. Organised by Association de Brocanteurs de Seine-et-Marne, 100 rue du Général de Gaulle, 77780 Bourron-Marlotte, telephone 60.70.14.95.

Mirande 32300

Salon des antiquaires de Mirande (Mirande antique dealers' salon) the last weekend of July throughout the village centre. This is a regional show, but discoveries of rustic items and country furniture sometimes can make it worthwhile. The date makes it a festive and entertaining (as well as heavily attended) show. Information from Les Amis du Passé, Hôtel des Pyrenees, 5 rue d'Etigny, 32300 Mirande, telephone 62.66.68.98.

Montauban 82000

Marché aux puces (flea market) every Saturday morning (early!) at place Prax-Paris, in the town centre. This market is part of the food and general merchandise market. Because this part of central France has never been very rich, you're likelier to find domestic and rustic farm items such as copper basins, fired clay jugs and casseroles, and some folk art than polished, stylish decorative pieces. Since traditional furniture of the region consists of heavy and massive pieces, you won't often find much of it at this market. Information from the Office de Tourisme, rue Collége Montauban, 82000 Montauban, telephone 63.63.60.60.

Salon des antiquaires et brocanteurs du Quercy (Quercy regional antique and junk dealers' salon) first Thursday to following Sunday of December at the Salle des Fêtes de Montauban. This fair is a good place to find regional furniture (measure the height before buying!) as well as small items of the region. Expert appraisers are on duty. Organised by GERM, 82000 Montauban, telephone 63.63.00.40, or Michel Gomez, 5 avenue du 11-RI, 82000 Montauban, telephone 63.03.23.34.

Mont-de-Marsan 40000

Marché aux puces (flea market) first Wednesday of every month year round at the place Saint-Roch, in the centre of town near rue Gambetta. This is a relatively small country-style market, worth seeing if you're in the area but not worth a special journey. Street parking is available at the railway station or at the car park on allées Brouchet. Information from the Office de Tourisme, 22 rue Victor Hugo, Boîte Postale 407,

40012 Mont-de-Marsan, telephone 58.75.38.67, telex 540742 F CDTLAND.

Montferrand 63100

(Please see Clermont-Ferrand.)

Montluçon 03100

Marché à la brocante (junk market) third Sunday of the month year round. Information from the Office de Tourisme, 1 ter, avenue Marx-Dormoy, 03100 Montluçon, telephone 70.06 05.92.

Montpellier 34000

Marché aux puces (flea market) every Sunday morning (beginning at dawn) year round at the Stade Richter, on the route de Carnon. This is one of the best markets in France and offers lots of old objects seemingly from the wine trade in addition to the the usual flea market bric-a-brac. You'll also find books—probably since the city is the home of an ancient university. Information from the Office de Tourisme, place Comédie, 34000 Montpellier, telephone 87.60.76.90. A branch tourist office is at the Gare S.N.C.F. (main railway station).

Foire aux anes (donkey market) first Monday of February and the beginning of November on the boulevard des Arceaux, about 1 kilometre west of the city centre. Organised by the Service des Marchés, Mairie de Montpellier, allée de la Citadelle, 34000 Montpellier.

Salon de l'antiquité et de la brocante (antique and junk salon) beginning about the 25th of April and continuing through the second Sunday of May at the Parc des Expositions in the Montpellier-Fréjorgues district. The day before the show is opened to the public is reserved for dealer sales—bring your business card and maybe a copy of your business licence. Over 100 exhibitors stay only for the dealers' day. This is the preeminent show of the region; about 200 dealers bring small art, including bronzes, glass, local books, and engravings. Large quantities of furniture and local arts are also for sale. Access is easy by car; parking is available at the site. Organised by A. Cipolat, 21 rue de la République, 30129 Manduel, telephone 66.20.02.19. Information is available from the fairgrounds, S.E.M.F.I.M., Boîte Postale 1056, 34006 Montpellier Cedex, telephone 67.64.12.12, telex 490805 F FIM.

Moret-sur-Loing 77250

(Please also see Bourron-Marlotte and Fontainebleau.)

Foire à la brocante (junk fair) first weekend of September in this small village made famous by the Impressionist painters of the late 19th century. About 70 vendors offer all types of antiques and collectables. Reproductions and altered goods are prohibited. Organised by the Association de Brocanteurs de Seine-et-Marne (A.B.S.E.M.), 100 rue du Général de Gaulle, 77780 Bourron-Marlotte, telephone 60.70.14.95.

Mouans-Sartoux 06370

Foire à la brocante (junk fair) third weekend of July (Saturday, Sunday, and Monday) all day every year at the square de la Poste. This Provençal village is just 10 kilometres from Cannes, on the Riviera. This is a major fair and is well worth attending if you're in the area. Organised by the Syndicat d'Initiative, telephone 93.75.51.99.

Nancy 54000

Marché aux puces (flea market) second Saturday of the month year round on the Grand' rue in the Old Town in the   city   centre.   This market, set among ancient overhanging buildings, is also one of the best markets in France. Lorraine is one of France's economically declining industrial areas, always a good sign when looking for antiques and collectables. Specialities of the region you may find include crystal by Baccarat and Daum, wood carvings and religious statues, chimney plaques, and faïence.

While you're at the market, see the place Stanislaus only a block away, which is one of the most beautiful ensembles of 18th-century civic architecture in the world.

Information from the Office de Tourisme, 14 place Stanislaus, Boîte Postale 803, 54011 Nancy Cedex, telephone 83.35.22.41, telex ESSINCY 960414.

Salon des antiquaires et de la brocante (antique dealers' and junk salon) during mid-April (check, because exact dates vary each year) at the Parc des Expositions, about 2 kilometres south of the city centre where boulevard Berthout turns into the autoroute. A major regional fair of around 100 dealers; plenty of parking is available on the site. Organised by M. Theux, Salon des Antiquaires, Parc des Expositions de Nancy, Boîte Postale 593, 54009 Nancy Cedex, telephone 83.51.09.01, fax 83.56.54.06, telex MIDEST 960596 F.

Nantes 44000

Marché aux puces, Saturday morning (early!) year round at place Viarme. The first weekend of May and last weekend of September or first weekend of October, this becomes one of the major markets of the autumn season. This large irregular square is about one kilometre north west of the Chateau and about 200 metres west of the main food and general market on rue Talensac. This market is one of the better and larger flea markets in France, where you may find Chinese porcelain, Delftware, and local faience and domestic pottery, and "LU" biscuit tins. Since Nantes is one of the major seaports of France, this market sometimes has quantities of foreign antiques (especially from England). Organised by M. Michel, 22 place Viarmes, 44000 Nantes. Information from the Office de Tourisme, Place du Commerce, 44000 Nantes, telephone 40.47.04.51.

Salles des Ventes (public auction halls) auctions every Monday, Wednesday, and Friday at 2 p.m. This is one of the major provincial auctions—well worth attending. Local specialities include furniture and maritime items. Inspection and buyer registration takes place during regular business hours and before the sale begins. Information and sale at Salles des Ventes, 6 rue Babonneau, 44000 Nantes, telephone 40.69.24.10.

Salon de l'antiquité (antiques salon) the third weekend of November at the Parc des Expositions in the parc de la Baujoire, just north of boulevard A. Fleming about four kilometres north of the city centre. This is a relatively new fair. Organised by the Foire International et Congrès de Nantes, Centre Neptune, 44000 Nantes, telephone 40.35.75.79.

Narbonne 11100

Marché aux puces (flea market) Thursday morning year round at place Voltaire. This small but interesting market specializes in folk art, local paintings, glass, and sometimes winegrowing equipment. At the beginning of July, the fair is extended through the weekend and is much larger and more interesting, with hundreds of buyers. Organised by the Service des Marchés, Ville de Narbonne, 11100 Narbonne, telephone 68.32.31.60. Information is also available from the Office de Tourisme, place R. Salengro, 11100 Narbonne, telephone 68.65.15.60.

Foire à la brocante (junk fair) the first half of July (check for exact dates) in the quartier Voltaire. This is a celebration as well as a market. Organised by the Comité Voltaire, Mairie de Narbonne, 11100 Narbonne, telephone 68.42.35.79.

Nice 06000

Marché de la brocante, livres, et friperie (junk, book, and used clothes market) every day except Sunday from 8 a.m. to 1 p. m. and 3 p.m. to 5 p.m. around the Port de Nice. This market consists of about 30 permanent vendors installed in sheds, selling all kinds of junk. Selection is acceptable but not grand; skilled and informed vendors make true finds rare, though the atmosphere is interesting. Note: this market was moved here due to construction on the Paillon, and may be moved from this location in the near future.

Parking is available on the street (though difficult to find) or underground under the central median of the boulevard. Organised by the Ville de Nice, Service des Marchés, Hôtel de Ville, 06000 Nice, telephone 93.13.20.00.

Marché à la brocante (junk market) every Monday year round on cours Saleya, in the old central city, with approximately 200 vendors. This is part of the colourful general merchandise, flower, and food market. Though you'll probably not make any great finds, you could find some Italian work, or neglected silver plate. Parking is available on the street (though difficult to find) or in an underground car park beneath cours Seleya. Organised by the Ville de Nice, Service des Marchés, Hôtel de Ville, 06000 Nice, telephone 93.13.20.00. Information from the Office de Tourisme, Acropolis, esplanade Kennedy, 06300 Nice, telephone 93.92.82.82, telex 461045 F.

La Promenade des antiquaires (antique dealers' gallery) open every day except Wednesday at 7 promenade des Anglais, is a gathering of about two dozen dealers offering quality coupled with relatively high prices. A pay parking garage is available nearby on the rue Massenet.

Nîmes 30000

Marché aux puces (flea market) every Monday year round on the Allée Jean-Jaurès near place

Jules Guesde. This market is in the median of a wide boulevard, and is next to a produce and plant market. Quality of used items is often poor, but if you look, you might find something interesting. Free street parking is ample, and a large car park is in place Jules Guisde. Toilets are non-existent.

Do not confuse this market with the Marché des Halles food market on the rue Général Perrier in the city centre, which has one of the finest food markets in France. Information from the Office de Tourisme, 6 rue Auguste, 30000 Nîmes, telephone 66.67.29.11, telex OFFITOUR NIMES 490926 F. Organised by Ville de Nîmes, Bureau Numéro 2113, Le chef de Service des Foires et Marchés, Hôtel de Ville, 30033 Nîmes Cedex, telephone 66.76.70.01.

Théatre de la Renaissance (Renaissance theatre) is the site of 30 permanent dealers in a recently restored Beaux- Arts theatre on the place des Carmes. Dealers offer all types of items, all older than 1930. This permanent establishment replaces the antiques market on the place des Carmes. Open every day from 10 a.m. to 7 p.m., closed on Wednesday and Thursday. Information and display at Théatre de la Renaissance, 5-7 place Gabriel Péri, 30000 Nîmes, telephone 66.76.26.46.

Salon des antiquaires et brocanteurs (antique and junk dealers' salon) the for 9 days in the first half of of December at the Parc des Expositions on rue de Bouillargues, on the eastern edge of the city. The two days before the salon is open to the public are reserved for members of the antiques trade: take a business card or copy of your business licence. About 150 dealers exhibit: this is one of the major regional markets in France. Specialities include 18th- and 19th-century furniture, bronzes, and art glass. Take rue de Bouillarges under the railway tracks from boulevard Talabot, the main street along the tracks; the Parc des Expositions is about 200 meters past the tunnel. There is also the journées nationales de la brocante (national junk days) at the same place at the end of March. Information from M. J.P. Mingaud, Salon des Antiquaires, Parc des

Expositions, rue de Bouillargues, 30000 Nîmes, telephone 66.84.93.39.

Salle des Ventes (public sales hall) auctions every Monday and Thursday at 9 a.m., offering ordinary used goods and collectables. In addition, there are special auctions of finer items and specialized collector's items most Saturdays. Saturday sales are announced in the Gazette de l'Hôtel Drouot, or you can request the schedule from the auction hall. Information from and sales at Salle des Ventes, 69 rue Nationale, 30000 Nîmes, telephone 66.67.52.74.

Niort 79000

Petit marché à la brocante (little flea market) first Wednesday of every month year round in the market hall in the centre of town along the river. This provincial town in central France offers only occasional finds. Information from the Office de Tourisme, place Poste, 79000 Niort, telephone 49.24.18.79.

Nogent-le-Rotrou 28400

Hôtel des Ventes du Perche (Perche public auction hall) auctions every Saturday year round and one Sunday per month at 2 p.m., with quantities of furniture from the 18th to 20th centuries. Inspection of merchandise and buyer registration is held before the sale. Information and sales at the Salle des Ventes, 13 rue Abbé-Beulé, 28400 Nogent-le-Rotrou, telephone 37.52.01.85.

Salon des antiquaires (antique dealers' salon) at the beginning of October at the Salle Polyvalente. This is a small local fair of minor interest. Organised by the Mairie de Nogent-le-Rotrou, rue Villette-Gaté, 28400 Nogent-le-Rotrou.

Nogent-sur-Marne 94130

Salon des antiquaires (antique dealers'salon) the third weekend of January (exact dates vary from year to year) at the Pavillon Baltard. This is a relatively new fair, but about 50 vendors offer good-quality antiques. Organised by Prom'Art, 11 impasse Beethoven, 35000 Rennes, telephone 99.50.74.19.

Nolay 21340

Foire à la brocante et aux antiquitàs (antique and junk fair) Easter Saturday, Sunday, and Monday, and the weekend of Assumption day (August 15) under the market hall. This is a small local fair. Organised by M. Monnot, 18 rue Sadi-Carnot, 21340 Nolay, telephone 80.21.72.99.

Obernai 67210

Foire à la brocante (junk fair) twice a year: the second Wednesday to Sunday of May and October 31 to November 2, at the Salle des Fêtes. Obernai is a picturesque town in Alsace; at the fair you'll find massive country furniture, blue pottery wine pitchers, and stoneware crocks, among other items. Information from M. Kleim, 21 place de l'Etoile, 67210 Obernai, telephone 88.95.52.80.

Orange 84100

Marché aux puces (flea market) every Thursday morning at the Place des Cordeliers. This market, which has only a few dealers in antiques and junk, is mainly a food and general merchandise market. Information from the Office de Tourisme, cours Aristide Briand, Boîte Postale 140, 84104 Orange Cedex, telephone 90.34.70.88, telex 432857.

Grande brocante d'Orange (grand junk fair of Orange) Easter weekend and Assumption day weekend (August 15) at the Palais de la Foire in

the Parc des Expositions, 100 metres from the
motorway junction. Each fair lasts from
Thursday through Sunday. This is a major
regional fair, with several hundred stands. Organised by Les Amis de la Brocante d'Orange, 4
rue Gabriel Boissy, 84100 Orange, telephone
90.34.71.89.

Orléans 45000

Marché aux puces (flea market) Saturday morning from about 7.30 a.m. on boulevard Alexandre
Martin, the wide boulevard near the railway station. This boulevard is on the site of the now-
demolished city walls. This market is part of the
regular food and general merchandise market,
and is worthwhile if you are in the area.

Street parking is available but difficult after
about 8.30 a.m. There are underground pay
parking garages directly under the marketplace.
Information from the Office de Tourisme, place
Albert   1er.,   45000   Orléans,   telephone
38.53.05.95, telex 781188.

Galerie des Ventes (public sales gallery) auctions
on variable dates during the year, but mostly in
February and March, May and June, and
November and December. The gallery is near the
railway bridge over the Loire on the east side of
the city. A list of dates and times is available
from the organiser, and a catalogue is available
before each sale. Dates and sales times are also
advertised in the Les Ventes Prochaines section
of Gazette de l'Hôtel Drouot. These sales offer
fine-quality antiques, particularly furniture. The
sales take place and information is available
from Galerie des Ventes, Mme. Savot, boulevard
Motte-Sanguin   (impasse   Notre-Dame   de
Chemin), 45000 Orléans, telephone 38.62.67.84.

Salon des antiquaires et de la brocante, (antique
dealers' and junk salon) second week of March at
the Parc des Expositions, rue du Président
Robert Schumann, about 2 kilometres south of
the Loire on the way to the Parc Floral (follow
the signs). An admission charge is made. This is
a major regional fair. Information from the Parc

des Expositions, 1 rue du Président Robert Schumann, Boîte Postale 5002, 45081 Orléans Cedex 2, telephone 38.66.28.20.

Foire à la brocante (junk fair) in mid-December on the quai de Prague, on the south bank of the Loire across from the city centre. Organised by the Direction de la Voierie, Hôtel de Ville, place Saint-Croix, 45000 Orléans.

Paris 75000

(Please also see Chatou, Chelles, Etampes, Nogent-sur-Marne, Samois-sur-Seine, Savigny-sur-Orge and Versailles.)

(Map of Paris on pages 125-125.)

Paris is the undisputed centre of the French antiques trade, just as it is the undisputed center of France in things ranging from government and finance to books and retailing. Few other countries in the world are as centralized as France. Few other cities of the world are as rich in antiques, flea markets, and auctions as Paris (except London).

The flea market may have originated in Paris, in part as the result of the 19th-century redesign of the city of Paris. This redesign forced the junk dealers and rag pickers to move outside the city gates. Once at the city gates of Paris, they stayed: even today the flea markets of Paris are at or near the city limits, conveniently (for motorists) near to the boulevard Périphérique ring expressway around Paris.

Weekends are when most flea markets in Paris are open, though there are antiques to be found every day of the week.

Antique Shops

There are hundreds if not thousands of antique and junk shops in Paris; there are pages of them in the telephone book (look under "Antiquités"). Most shops seem to be centered in several districts: the Left Bank, near Saint-Germain-des-

Pres, along rue Saint-Honoré, and near the Hôtel Drouot. Walk along the streets of any of these neighborhoods: you'll be attracted to antique shops as delectable as sweet shops to children of all ages.

Paris Flea Markets

Porte de Clignancourt—Saint-Ouen, Saturday, Sunday and Monday from dawn to about an hour before dusk. Early Saturday morning is the best time to find the new items; Monday afternoon is the best time to bargain with the dealers.

Clignancourt is the original, prototypical flea market, which has been in existence for much more than a century. In this period, it has grown from small to large to gigantic: it may be the largest single concentration of junk and antiques for sale in the world.

It is actually formed of six independently owned markets (Paul Bert, Biron, Cambo, Serpette, Jules Vallès, and Vernaison) within a few blocks of each other. Each has a different atmosphere and different specialities, but since they're all in the same neighborhood, they can be treated together. Each has between 80 and 300 stall holders (about 1200 in all) who open up late in the morning, from about 9.30 to as late as 11.30 a.m.

Probably 100 independent street merchants work out of suitcases, card tables, and cardboard boxes. They arrive early and usually are gone by 10.30, which is when the permanent booth holders in the established markets are just arriving and opening.

Remember as you work the alleys that all of these dealers are professionals and usually know the value of the merchandise. Though finds can occasionally be made, don't expect a long-lost painting by Watteau or Fragonard.

Parking is difficult on market day after about 7.30; there is street parking on the rue René Binet and surrounding streets. A pay parking garage is at the corner of avenue de la Porte de Clignancourt and rue de F. Croisset, but will often be full after about 9.30 in the morning.

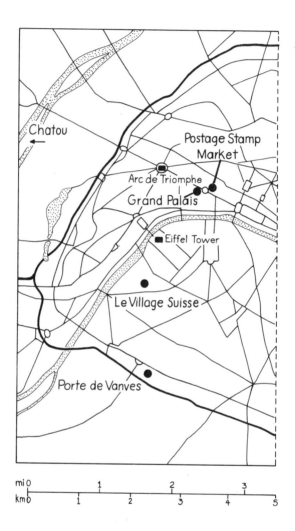

Chatou

Postage Stamp Market

Arc de Triomphe

Grand Palais

Eiffel Tower

Le Village Suisse

Porte de Vanves

mi 0   1   2   3
km 0   1   2   3   4   5

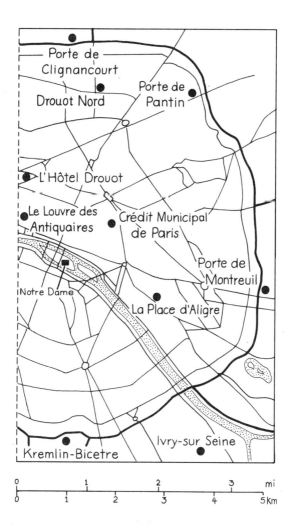

Porte de
Clignancourt

Drouot Nord

Porte de
Pantin

L'Hôtel Drouot

Le Louvre des
Antiquaires

Crédit Municipal
de Paris

Porte de
Montreuil

Notre Dame

La Place d'Aligre

Ivry-sur Seine

Kremlin-Bicetre

0   1   2   3   mi
0   1   2   3   4   5 Km

Access by Metro to the Porte de Clignancourt station (end of the line) and walk under the underpass. The market is centred on the rue des Rosiers, the first diagonal street on your left, just past the underpass. You can also take bus 56 to the boulevard Périphérique.

See the map of the area on the facing page.

Porte de Vanves, Saturday and Sunday from dawn to 5 p.m. on the school side of avenue Marc Sangnier and on avenue Georges Lafenestre between avenue Marc Sangnier to the bridge over the boulevard Périphérique. The market is on the southern edge of Paris, best before about 10 a.m. Furniture tends to be found on avenue Marc Sangnier; everything else is found throughout the market.

This market seems to be where Parisians go; you'll find all kinds of items of good quality, and reasonable prices. About 200 vendors, some full-time professionals and some apparently part-time collectors, sell at this market. Some dealers from the Clignancourt market make their purchases here, then double the price for the tourists.

When it is not raining, you'll often see lots of massive pieces of furniture. On any day you'll find silver, silver plate, books, and crystal and glass. There are few clothes, and no food. No public toilets are to be found.

The market takes place in the street on avenue Georges Lafenestre and on the sidewalk along avenue Marc Sangier. There are no permanent vendors.

Street parking can be found on the street, but may require early arrival or a frantic search. There are no garages closer than the pay parking one along the railway tracks on the other side of the boulevard Périphérique.

Access by Metro to Porte de Vanves, then walk a short way south (toward the Pèriphèrique, which is underground) to avenue Marc Sangnier. You should see the vendors about halfway down the block.

Porte de Montreuil, Sunday morning from about 7 a.m. until just after noon. Access by Metro to the Porte de Montreuil station, then continue out (east) from the subway exit across the boulevard

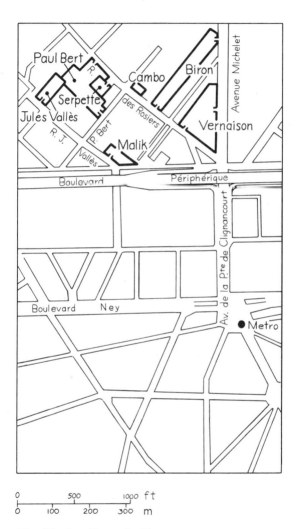

Flea Market, Porte de Clignancourt, Paris

Périphérique. Just past the circle, you'll see the
market on your left sandwiched between the ring
road and the avenue du Professeur André
Lemierre.

About 200 vendors of new and used clothes,
kitchen gadgets, and lots of bric-a-brac cram into
a tiny space. About a third of the vendors sell
used items, little furniture but lots of broken
items and anonymous junk. This is a lower-class
neighbourhood, and the merchandise reflects the
neighborhood's poverty.

Parking is available on surrounding streets,
though you'll have to look. There are no parking
garages in the neighbourhood.

La place d'Aligre, Tuesday to Sunday (especially
on Sunday) from early morning to about 1 p.m.
This market is hard to find, hidden away in the
run-down eastern 12th Arrondisement.

This market has an abundance of cheap new
and used clothes, food and vegetables, and about
20 to 40 dealers in junk, bric-a- brac, and some
battered furniture. While the choice is not as
great as some other markets, prices are probably
the lowest in Paris.

Parking is available on the street, but you will
have to search for a space.

Access by Metro to the Ledru-Rollin station,
then walk east along rue du Faubourg
Saint-Antoine to avenue d'Aligre. Turn right and
a short way along you'll see the market hall on
your left (food and drink except on Sunday) and
about 40 junk dealers in the square.

Kremlin-Bicetre, Tuesday, Thursday, and Sunday
from early morning to about noon on avenue
Eugene-Thomas (Porte d'Italie). The market, in a
rather grimy working-class neighbourhood, is
further along: it is partly in the main boulevard
and partly on side streets. Hundreds of vendors
mostly sell assorted odds and ends; maybe you'll
find something, but it is not as likely as at the
markets listed above.

Parking on the street is possible, but you'll
probably have to walk a short distance.

Access by Metro to the Porte d'Italie station,
then walk south across the boulevard
Périphérique.

Porte de Pantin, Marché des Greniers de France, Friday, Saturday, and Sunday mornings (best around 8.30 a. m.). The market has the normal array of bric-a-brac, collectables, and sometimes furniture woven into a fabric of food, clothes, and kitchen gadgets made of plastic, wood, and metal. This is a relatively minor market, and should not be your first choice.

Parking on the street is relatively easy to find compared to most of Paris.

Access by Metro to Porte de Pantin.

Postage stamp market, Thursday afternoons and all day Sunday on avenue Gabriel and avenue Marigny, across the street from the Elysées Palace, residence of the President of France.

This is a specialized market strictly devoted to postage stamps. While dozens of dealers and collectors set up tables along the sidewalk and on the gravel and you can find stamps from all over the world, it is unlikely you'll find stamps of great value and rarity.

Street parking in this neighborhood is almost impossible. Public parking is available in the garage on avenue Marigny, just off the Rond-Point des Champs-Elysées.

Access by Metro to the Champs-Elysées-Clemenceau station, then walk a little way on avenue de Marigny.

Paris Auctions

L'Hôtel Drouot (Hotel Drouot), formally known as the Nouveau Drouot, is France's largest set of auction halls, and is also the centre of a sizeable area of experts, appraisers, shippers, and dealers. There are several auctions almost every day of the week in some of the 16 auction halls the Nouveau Drouot.

The entire complex is open from 11 a.m. to 6 p.m. Monday through Saturday; closed Sunday and the entire month of August.

Many French (and foreign) antique dealers buy their goods here (also less artistic items are sometimes sold here as well, such as appliances, used furniture, even, occasionally, industrial equipment!). Usually, buyer registration before the sale is required. Payment is required in French francs, either in cash or by cheque. A buyer's premium is payable in addition to the sales price. The premium is 17.674% on the first 15,000 francs, 13.2265% on sales from 15,001 to 40,000 francs, 11.151% on sales from 40,001 to 300,000 francs, and 9.965% on all sales over 300,000 francs.

Many sales are specialized categories: paintings, carpets, furniture, and silver. However, many sales are miscellaneous lots of some furniture, a few paintings, a few glass or crystal items, and other similar collectable or antique items.

Announcements of coming sales are published every Friday in the weekly La Gazette de l'Hôtel Drouot, which is available at the newsstand just inside to the right of the main entrance. Some newsstands in the neighbourhood also carry it.

For the schedule of coming sales, you can call a 24-hour recording (in French only) at 47.70.17.17. You can also see a schedule on Teletel (French national computer videotext system) by calling 36.15.91.77 and typing GDROUOT on the keyboard.

Most sales begin at 2 p.m.; inspection of merchandise is usually held the day before from the opening of the doors at 11 a.m. to 5 p.m. (7 p.m. on Thursday), and sometimes also on the day of the sale from 11 a.m. until noon.

In addition to the auctions, many services necessary for the antique trade are found in the building and in the neighbourhood: shippers, experts and appraisers (some of whom can be of great help when exporting works of art and antiques).

The Hôtel Drouot is located at 9 rue Drouot, Paris 75009, telephone 42.46.17.11, telex Drouot 642260. Rue Drouot runs between rue La Fayette and boulevard Montmartre.

Parking is extremely difficult in the vicinity; however, the nearest parking garage (pay) is at the back of the building and entered at 12 rue Chauchat.

The closest Metro stops are Le Peletier, Richelieu-Drouot, and Notre-Dame de Lorette.

Bus lines passing nearby are 20, 39, 42, 48, 67, 74, and 85.

Drouot Nord, a smaller auction hall on the north side of Paris, consists of three salesrooms. This is finds can be made, but not all items are antiques. Most sales are of all types of miscellaneous goods mixed into the same sales, including old furniture, reproductions, office equipment, even some items such as new factory samples, and used electronic goods. Finds can be made here, but it takes patience.

Most sales begin at 9 a.m. every day from Monday to Friday. Inspection and registration takes place the 15 minutes before the sale begins each day.

The schedule of the buyer's premium is exactly the same as at the main salesrooms on rue Drouot.

Drouot Nord is at 64 rue Doudeauville, 75018 Paris, telephone (1) 42.62.39.99.

Access by Metro is to Marcadet-Poissoniers or Château Rouge. Access by bus is on lines 31, 56, 60, 65, and 85. Parking is available in the car park: the entrance is at 23 rue d'Oran.

Crédit Municipal de Paris (municipal pawn shop) holds regular auctions to dispose of pawned and unclaimed items. Quality is variable; you will have to inspect carefully. Sales are organised into categories such as jewellery, books, musical instruments, and "divers"—which means everything else. More sales consist of jewellery (which includes silver, silverware, gold and silver coins, and rings, necklaces, etc.) than anything else. The sales are held at 10.30 a.m. unless otherwise specified in advertising (found in La Gazette de l'Hôtel Drouot and elsewhere), but the days vary. No auctions are held in August. Information can be obtained from the sale site, Crédit Municipal de Paris, 55 rue des Francs-Bourgeois, 75181 Paris Cedex 04, telephone 42.71.25.43.

Parking in the area is extremely difficult; the nearest parking garages are found near the Beaubourg (Pompidou Center). Enter from the rue de Beaubourg.

The closest Metro stop is Rambuteau, then walk east away from the Pompidou Centre.

Antiques Centres

Le Louvre des antiquaires (antique dealers' Louvre) is an antique dealers' and antique collectors' dream, though not by any means a flea market. This massive four-storey old building was originally opened in 1855 as one of the world's first department stores. After closing as a department store, it reopened with about 250 dealers of some of the most exquisite (and costly) antiques to be found. Not only are the displays wonderful, the setting is classic: a fine skylighted centre with silent escalators, polished hardwood floors, soothing music, and clean, free public toilets (south east corner, second floor). Any dealer here should be able to authenticate any item you buy. Even if you can't afford to buy anything, it is a worthwhile browse. The Louvre des antiquaires open every day except Monday from 11 a.m. to 7 p.m. at 2 place du Palais-Royal, 75044 Paris Cedex 01, telephone 42.97.27.00. (Across rue de Rivoli on one side is the Louvre and on the other side across the rue Saint-Honoré is the information office that deals with the exportation of artwork and antiques.)

Parking is almost impossible, though you can on rare occasions find a place to park at the few metred spaces in the square.

Access by Metro is to the Palais Royal station, then walk across the square.

Le Village Suisse (Swiss Village) is another elegant complex of about 150 dealers, on the Left Bank only a short walk from the Eiffel Tower. The shops in this relatively new concrete complex are tiny, but have many exquisite pieces, some of which are of museum quality. Prices here are also quite high and you should be able to obtain certificates of authenticity on almost any purchase made here. This complex is open Thursday to Monday from 11 a.m. to 7 p.m., though because of the layout, you can window-shop on any day of the week. Le Village Suisse has two entrances and two addresses: 78 avenue de Suffren and (around the corner) 54 avenue de la Motte-Picquet.

This is one area of Paris where you may be able to find street parking.

Access by Metro is to the Motte-Picquet or Grenelle stations, then walk a little way down the avenue de la Motte-Picquet. Every stand has its own telephone number: there is no central information number.

Antique Shows

There are several antique shows in Paris (see also surrounding town listings). The major shows in Paris are listed here.

Biennale internationale des antiquaires (international antique dealers' biennial) from the third week of September to the second Sunday of October of even numbered years. It is held at the Grand Palais on the Champs-Elysées at place Clemenceau. This is the largest and most elegant antique show in France. Several hundred antique dealers, mostly French but with a sprinkling of foreign dealers, display all kinds of antiques. Almost all items are of museum quality.

Parking can be difficult. The nearest public parking lot is at the Rond-Point des Champs Elysées, with the entrance on avenue Matignon.

Access by Metro is to the Champs-Elysées Clemenceau station, then walk toward the Seine to find the main entrance. Organised by the French National Antiques Dealers Association, Syndicat National des Antiquaires, 11 rue Jean-Mermoz, 75008 Paris, telephone 42.25.44.33.

Foire nationale à la brocante
(Please see Chatou.)

Foire internationale à la brocante et de l'antiquité (international junk and antiques fair) the last week of February and last week of September It is held at the Parc des Cormailles just outside Paris' city limits in Ivry-sur-Seine. It is one of the largest antiques fairs in France, and coincides with the Chatou fair and the bienniale in even-numbered years. Over 1000 dealers show all kinds of antiques and collectables ranging from glassware and silver plate to furniture. The first two days are reserved for the antiques trade: have a business card or copy of your business licence ready. This fair is definitely worth attending.

Access by Metro to the end of the line at the Mairie d'Ivry, then follow the signs and walk downhill to the railway station. Access by RER on Line C to Ivry-sur-Seine (the first station past the city boundary; costs a few francs). Ample parking is available at the fair site.

Information from Mme. Micheline Resse, SODAF, 18 rue Lénine (2 place des Fauconnières), 94200 Ivry-sur-Seine, telephone (1) 46.71.66.14.

Other Events and Organisers

In addition, about two dozen events are organised by several companies and organizations. Since these markets are subject to change from year to year, contact them when you arrive in France. Generally, they are street fairs, though some are held in various halls and stadiums. These organizations are:

- SADEMA Société d'Animation et Diffusion des Ensembles Modernes et Anciens, 47 boulevard Blanqui, 75013 Paris, telephone 45.65.95.95. This company organises about 10 fairs per year, including brocante de Paris (junk of Paris) at the Square de Kouffra (14th arrondisement) in mid to late January, the brocante de Paris et salon des papieres anciens et des collections (junk of Paris and alon of ancient and collectable papers) at the Espace Champerret (Halls A and C) during the second week of February, the farraille de Paris (iron of Paris, includes junk) at the end of paris in the Parc de Floral de Paris in the Bois de Vincennes, the foire de brocante de printemps (spring junk fair) held on at the square des Batignolles (17th arrondisement), around the end of May; foires de brocante (junk fairs) held at the place Baudoyer (4th arrondisement) during early May, at place de la Bastille (4th arrondisement) at the end of May, and on avenue du Maine (14th arrondisement) in early June, brocante de Paris (Paris junk) at Boulogne-sur-Seine, dates vary; and the salon d'antiquaires (antique dealers' salon) at on quai Branly at the end of November and beginning of December, or in Fontainebleau in odd-numbered years.

- O. G. S., 96 rue des Rosiers, 93400 Saint-Ouen, telephone (1) 42.62.44.44. This company organises two huge junk fairs a year, the Foire à la Ferraille et aux Jambons (used iron and ham fair), held in March and in September at the Parc Floral de Paris in the Bois de Vincennes.

- Arts-Expo, 10 rue Thénard, 75005 Paris, telephone 46.34.05.80. This company organises several specialized salons, such as the paintings and posters fair, held in April, and the salon des antiquaires, held at the end of November and beginning of December.

- M. Max Blaise, 153 rue de la Université, 75007 Paris, telephone 45.51.82.42. This organiser sponsors several fairs a year, including the bienniale des Anneés 1900-1950 (biennial fairs of items from 1900-1950), held at the Théâtre Chaillot in the autumn of even-numbered years, and a salon de l'antiquité (antiques salon) at the Musé3 Jacquemart André during the second half of March, plus some in the provinces.

Pau 64000

Marché à la brocante (junk market) every Saturday from 7 a.m. to 12 noon and 2 to 6 p.m., and every Sunday from 9 a.m. until noon at the place de Foirail. This market is in one of the most lovely of French provincial cities, not far from the Pyrenees. You'll find items such as faïence from Samadet, items from nearby Spain, and clay jugs and pots of various types. Information from the Office de Tourisme, place Royale, 64000 Pau, telephone 59.27.27.08.

Salon des antiquaires (antique dealers' salon) in mid-February (check for exact dates) at the Parc des Expositions. This is a small local fair. For information contact the Mairie de Pau, rue Henri-IV, 64000 Pau.

Périgueux 24000

Hôtel des Ventes (public sales hall) auction every Wednesday at 2 p.m. Auctions include all types of used goods and furniture. Inspection and buyer registration is the morning of the sale from 9 a.m. to noon. Information and sales are held at the Hôtel des Ventes, 9 rue Bodin, 24000 Périgueux, telephone 53.08.60.84.

Salon des antiquaires (antique dealers' salon) for about a week around Easter. This is a recently established event. For exact details, contact M. Anne, Village Périgord, 39 avenue Charles de Gaulle, 24000 Périgueux, telephone 53.09.83.69.

Perpignan 66000

Marché aux puces (flea market) early Sunday morning year round at the Parc des Expositions on the avenue de Bompas, the riverbank street across from the city centre. This is probably the largest market on the southern Mediterranean coast, with over 150 regular vendors, but often the merchandise is disappointing. Look for forged iron work, domestic clay pottery (especially jugs) bronze statues, and, occasionally, faïence plates. Information from the Office Municipal de Tourisme, Palais des Congrès, place Armand Lanoux, Boòte Postale 215, 66000 Perpignan, telephone 68.34.13.13, telex 500500 F.

Foire de brocante et antiquités (junk and antique fair) first Saturday of the month at the promenade de Platanes on the south side of the river. Though this is a smaller fair than the Sunday fair, better-quality merchandise is for sale, with some of the local specialities such as clay pottery. Information from the Office Municipal de Tourisme, Palais des Congrès, place Armand

Lanoux, Boîte Postale 215, 66000 Perpignan, telephone 68.34.13.13, telex 500500 F.

Salon des antiquaires du Roussillon (Roussillon antique dealers' salon) at Easter and in October (call for exact dates) at the 14th-century Chapelle Saint-Dominique on rue Rabelais. This is a smaller and newer fair than many provincial fairs, mainly featuring local dealers with quantities of 19th-century furniture. Organised by the Groupement des Antiquaires et Brocanteurs du Roussilon, 11 rue Alart, 66000 Perpignan, telephone 68.55.49.42.

Pézenas 34120

Marché aux puces (flea market) every Wednesday morning year round at the place Gambetta. In mid-July and August, the market gets larger and the antique dealers move to where tourists can easily find them at the place du Marché-au-Bled in the town centre in front of the church. This small but ancient town invites antiques to surface. Wine-related items are common, since Pézenas is in the largest (if not most famous) wine-growing area of France. Organised by the Mairie de Pézenas, telephone 67.98.14.15. Information from M. Jean Servieres, Office de Tourisme, 3 rue A.P. Allieès, 34120 Pézenas, telephone 67.98.11.82.

Poitiers 86000

Marché aux puces (flea market) every Friday morning (early!) in the place du Marché square around the Notre-Dame le Grand church. This is the only flea market in the area, and is mixed in with the weekly food and general merchandise market. It is larger on the first Friday of the month. Specialities you might find include copper basins, and regional ceramics, mostly clay, but including some porcelain. Information from the Office de Tourisme, 8 rue des Grandes Ecoles, 86000 Poitiers, telephone 49.41.21.24, telex 702091 F.

On Pentecost Sunday and the following Monday (five weeks after Easter Sunday, usually in May) and the second Sunday and Monday of December the foire à la brocante (junk fair) is held at the same location. Information from the Office de Tourisme or from the organiser, M. Amédée Brousseau, rue de Vendeuvre, 86170 Neuville-de-Poitou, telephone 49.51.36.14.

Salon des antiquaires (antique dealers' salon) third weekend of October (including Friday) at the Parc des Expositions, which is about 2 kilometres east of the city centre in the direction of Limoges, and fronting on rue Salvador Allende. This is a regional fair, with a few dealers from outside the region. Information from M. Bernard Cotto, Association des Antiquaires et Negociants en Oeuvres d'Art du Poitou, 27 rue Carnot, 86000 Poitiers, telephone 49.58.20.17.

Pontault-Combault 77340

(Please also see Nogent-sur-Marne and Paris.)

Foire aux antiquités (antiques fair) second weekend of October at the Centre Carrefour. About 35 dealers offer all types of large and small antiques, including furniture. Modern reproductions, and mutilated or reworked old pieces are prohibited. Organised by Association de Brocanteurs de Seine-et-Marne, 100 Rue du Général de Gaulle, 77780 Bourron-Marlotte, telephone 60.70.14.95.

Pont-de-Vaux 01190

Marché aux puces (flea market) first Sunday of every month in the village centre. This is a small local market. Information from the Office de Tourisme, 1 rue Maréchal de Lattre-de-Tassigny, 01190 Pont-de-Vaux, telephone 85.37.30.02.

Pontoise 95300

Salle des Ventes (public sales hall) auction every
Monday and also the last Saturday of every
month at 2.30 p.m. The items run to 19th-cen-
tury furniture and minor paintings, as well as
normal glass and porcelain items. Inspection and
buyer registration is held the day before and on
the morning before the sale. Information from
and sales location is Salle des Ventes, 3 bis rue
Saint-Martin, 95300 Pontoise, telephone
30.31.01.83.

Pont Saint-Esprit 30130

Foire des antiquités et brocante (antique and
junk fair) first weekend of July (beginning
Friday) at place Saint-Pierre along the Quai de
Luynes on the Rhone river in the old town
centre. Organised by the Comité des Fêtes An-
tiquités-Brocante, Mairie, 30130 Pont Saint-
Esprit, telephone 66.39.09.80.

Salon des antiquités (antique salon) the four-day
weekend around Armistice Day (November 11) at
the Salle des Fêtes. This fair's vendors are mostly local and regional dealers with interesting
glass, porcelain, but only a small amount of furniture. A small admission fee is charged. Organised by the Comité des Fêtes Antiquités-
Brocante, Mairie, 30130 Pont Saint-Esprit,
telephone 66.39.09.80 or 66.39.44.45.

Pont-sur-Yonne 89140

Foire aux antiquités (antiques fair)· third
weekend of November in this small Burgundian
town. About 35 dealers offer all types of large
and small antiques, including furniture. Modern
reproductions and mutilated or reworked old
pieces are prohibited. Organised by Association
de Brocanteurs de Seine-et-Marne, 100 Rue du
Général de Gaulle, 77780 Bourron-Marlotte,
telephone 60.70.14.95.

Pornic 44210

Marché aux puces (flea market) every Thursday morning from the end of June to the beginning of September at Sainte-Marie-de-sur-Mer, just a mile west along the shore from Pornic. This is a small local market, with about 25 vendors fo furniture, books, old post cards, old clothes, and other items. Organised by Mme. Lemercker, Association Brocante et Curiosetés, Le Porteau, Sainte-Marie-sur-Mer, 44210 Pornic, telephone 40.82.07.29.

Brocante et curiosités (junk and curiosities) the first Sunday of August at the parking lot of the Salle Municipale. This small village near Nantes offers a local sale with some interesting items. Organised by Mme. Lemercker, Association Brocante et Curiosetés, Le Porteau, Sainte-Marie-sur-Mer, 44210 Pornic, telephone 40.82.07.29.

Provins 77160

Marché aux puces (flea market) third Sunday of every month year round at the place du Châtel in the partially walled Ville Haute (old upper town). Information from the Office de Tourisme, Tour César, Boîte 44, 77160 Provins, telephone 64.00.16.65, or the Comité d'Animation et d'Expansion Artistique, place du Châtel, 77160 Provins.

Foire aux antiquités (antiques fair) the last weekend of January. About 35 dealers offer all types of large and small antiques, including furniture. Modern reproductions and mutilated or reworked old pieces are prohibited. Organised by Association de Brocanteurs de Seine-et-Marne, 100 Rue du Général de Gaulle, 77780 Bourron-Marlotte, telephone 60.70.14.95.

Puy 43000

(Please see Le Puy.)

Quimper 29000

Salle des Ventes (public sales hall) auction every Wednesday at 2 p.m. Inspection and bidder registration is in the morning between 9 and 12 a.m. Information and sales at the Salle des Ventes, 7 boulevard de Kerguélen, 29000 Quimper, telephone 98.95.08.93.

Reims 51100

Marché aux puces (flea market) first Sunday of the month (except not in August) from 8 a.m. to 6 p.m. at Hall 3 in the Parc des Expositions in the Zone Industriel les Issillards, on R.N. 44 on the road to Châlons-sur-Marne. This market, with about 120 vendors, offers small collectable trinkets. Reproductions are prohibited. There is no admission charge and plenty of free parking. Access from the autorout at the Reims-Cormontriuil junction. Information from the organiser, Art Com' Riems, Boîte Postale 2014, 51070 Reims Cedex, telephone 26.02.00.13.

Marché aux puces (flea market) every Sunday year round on avenue Jean-Jaurés near boulevard Jamin, about 800 meters from the city centre on the road to Rethel. This is a food and general merchandise market, whose antique and flea market section is smaller than the once-a-month market. Organised by the city, Service des Marchés, Mairie de Reims, telephone 26.40.54.53, poste (extension) 1431. Information from the Office de Tourisme, 2 rue Guillaume de Marchault, Boîte Postale 2533, 51051 Reims cedex, telephone 26.47.25.46.

Salon des antiquaires (antique dealers' salon) the second half of October at the Parc des Expositions. This is a good regional fair, held at the Foire et Salons de Reims. Organised by the Société d'Exploitation du Parc des Expositions, Site Henri Farman, Boîte 2727, 51057 Reims Cedex, telephone 26.82.30.30, telex PARC EX 842630 F.

Salle des Ventes (public sales hall) auctions every Tuesday at 2 p.m. Inspection and buyer registration take place the morning of the sale. Information from and sales at Salle des Ventes, 31 rue Chativesle, 51100 Reims, telephone 26.47.26.37.

Remiremont 88200

Foire brocante champêtre (outdoors junk fair) in the town centre the first weekend of August. This is one of the largest weekend fairs in the eastern part of France and is well worth attending. Hundreds of vendors offer all types of antiques, junk, and used goods of all types. Organised by Mme. Marie-Jeanne Parmentier, la Lanterne, 22 rue de la Xavée, 88200 Remiremont, telphone 29.62.24.36.

Rennes 35000

Marché aux puces (flea market) every Thursday morning at the central market hall on the place des Lices. The main city of Brittany is a centre for furniture restoration and a treasure trove of unrestored furniture, particularly large dark 19th-century pieces such as armoires (which are often more than 8 feet high).

Marché aux puces Rennaises (Rennes flea market) the last week of January at the Salle Omnisports on boulevard de la Liberté. This is a major winter market with hundreds of dealers. Organised by Prom'Art, 11 impasse Beethoven, 35000 Rennes, telephone 99.50.74.19.

Salon des antiquaires (antique dealers' salon) last weekend of September at the Salle Omnisports on the boulevard de la Liberté. This is a large regional show. Organised by Prom'art, 11 impasse Beethoven, 35000 Rennes, telephone 99.50.74.19.

Rochelle

(Please see La Rochelle.)

Roche-sur-Yon 85000

Marché aux puces (flea market) second Sunday
of every month at the central market hall near
the Eglise Saint-Louis. Information from the Office de Tourisme, place Napoléon, 85000 Roche-
sur-Yon, telephone 74.36.09.63, telex 700784 F.

Romans-sur-Isère 26100

Marché à la brocante (junk market) first Saturday of every month at the place Charles de
Gaulle, at the foot of the Jacquemart tower in the
town centre. The regular food and general merchandise market (no antiques) is held at the
same location, but on Tuesday, Friday, and Sunday morning. Information from the Office de
Tourisme, Le Neuilly, place Jean Jaurés, Boîte
Postale 13, 26100 Romans-sur-Isère, telephone
75.02.28.72.

Roubaix 59100

(Please also see Lille.)

Marché aux puces (flea market) every Sunday
from 9 a.m. to noon at the parking garage in rue
du Général Serrail. This market, in a grimy brick
factory town almost on the Belgian border, has
about 50 sellers (more when it rains, because the
market is indoors) and is worth visiting after the
larger marché de Wazemmes in nearby Lille.
Similar items are sold. Information from Services Techniques, Ville de Roubaix, 59100
Roubaix, telephone 20.73.92.05.

Marché aux puces (flea market) every Saturday
morning at place E. Roussel in the Epeule district. This is a minor local market, but finds can
be made here. Information from Services Techniques, Ville de Roubaix, 59100 Roubaix, telephone
20.73.92.05.

Rouen 76000

The capital city of the opulent province of Normandy, Rouen is rich in antiques and collectables as well as old half-timbered houses and an ancient astronomical clock. It is a region still rich in many types of antiques, though sellers usually know the value of what they sell.

Marché aux puces (flea market) every Saturday and Sunday (early!) at the Clos Saint-Marc, near the church of Saint-Maclou in the city centre. This is the largest market in the area with about 100 vendors. You're likely to find various bibelots and collectables. This is part of the largest public market (some of which is indoors) in Rouen. In formation from the Office de Tourisme, 25 place Cathédrale, Boîte Postale 666, 76008 Rouen Cedex, telephone 35.71.41.77, telex 770940.

Marché aux puces (flea market) every Thursday morning at place des Emmurées. This is part of a regular food and general merchandise market and is less interesting than the other regular markets because there are fewer antiques. Information from the Office de Tourisme, 25 place Cathédrale, Boîte Postale 666, 76008 Rouen Cedex, telephone 35.71.41.77.

Foire à la ferraille (junk iron fair) in June (call for exact dates) on the rue de Robec and most of the Saint-Maclou district. This fair, which offers far more than junk iron, is the one of the largest flea markets in France. Hundreds of vendors offer both used and old goods and new items as well. Information is available from the organiser, C.C.C.R., telephone 35.70.98.50.

Salon des antiquaires de la Halle aux Toiles (antique dealers' salon) at the end of April and beginning of May (dates shift slightly from year to year) from 2 to 10 p.m., except 10 a.m. to 10 p.m. on weekends and May Day (May 1, a national holiday). It takes place at the Halle aux Toiles. About 100 dealers, mainly from the region, offer much of the best of fruitwood furniture, glass, crystal, faience, pottery, and silver. All items are antiques. Prices match the relatively high quality. Information from the organiser, Mme. Popelin, Association d'Antiquaires et Brocanteurs de Haute-Normandie, 20 rue Saint-Romain, 76000 Rouen, telephone 35.71.35.06.

Salon national des antiquaires (national antique dealers' salon) from the second to the third week of October at the Parc des Expositions. This is one of the major antique shows in France, with a regional emphasis. Some Parisian dealers also exhibit and buy at this fair. Prices are high but only true antiques (mostly of high quality) are sold. Information from the Groupe des Salons Sélectionées d'Antiquaires, boulevard de Champagne, Boîte Postale 108, 21003 Dijon Cedex, telephone 80.71.44.34, or the local organiser, M. Asseline, COMET, Boîte Postale 1135, 76175 Rouen Cedex, telephone 35.66.52.52.

Royan 17200

Marché de la brocante (junk market) every Wednesday and Sunday morning of July and August at La Tache Vert. This summer market is put on for the pleasure of the thousands of tourists flocking to this summer seaside resort. Information from the Office de Tourisme, Palais des Congrès (near the yacht harbour) 17200 Royan, telephone 46.38.65.11.

Royat 63130

(Please see Clermont-Ferrand.)

Sables d'Olonne 85100

(Please see Les Sables d'Olonne.)

Saint-Amand-Montrond 18200

Marché aux puces (flea market) the second Saturday of every month at the place du Marché. This is a small regional market. Only dealers may sell here; private parties may not. Information from the Office de Tourisme, place République, 18200 Saint-Amand-Montrond, telephone 48.96.16.86.

Saint-Brieuc 22000

Nouvel Hôtel des Ventes (new public auction hall) auction every Tuesday at 2 p.m. Registration Saturday, Monday, and just before the sale begins. This auction is one of the better places to buy old Breton furniture, old books, and nautical items. Catalogues are sometimes available several weeks before the most important sales. Information from the Nouvel Hôtel des Ventes, 10-12 rue de Gouët, 22000 Saint-Brieuc, telephone 96.33.15.91.

Foire à la brocante et aux antiquités (antique and junk fair) the last weekend of November or first weekend of December (including Friday) at the Parc de Brézillet. This is a regional fair, where you may find Breton antiques. Information from the Foire des Côtes d'Armor, Boîte Postale 236, Parc de Brézillet, 22004 Saint-Brieuc Cedex, telephone 96.94.04.13.

Saint-Ètienne 42000

Marché aux puces (flea market) every Sunday morning year round (starts early) on boulevard Jules-Janin, near the railway viaduct, Gare Saint-Ètienne Chateaucreux, and the Parc des Expositions on the north side of the city. This is the largest flea market in this part of central France; you're likely to find faïence and domestic pottery, open copper basins and especially iron cauldrons, andirons, and fireplace pokers. Information from the Office de Tourisme, 12 rue Gérentet, 42000 Saint-Ètienne, telephone 77.25.12.14 (closed Sunday).

Marché à la brocante (junk market) first Sunday of every month year round in the old city centre (vielle ville) Organised by the Association Promotion Brocante, 3 place Grenette, 42000 Saint-Ètienne, telephone 77.32.66.46.

Salon en Forez des antiquaires et brocanteurs (Forez antique and junk dealers' salon) for 10 days at the beginning of November at the Palais des Expositions on boulevard Jules-Janin. During the rest of the year, many of these dealers have permanent galleries, at which information can be obtained. Contact M. Patrick Verney-Carron, Groupement d'Intérêt Economique Antiquaires de Forez, rue de la Richelandière, 42100 Saint-Ètienne, telephone 77.32.65.49,

Hôtel des Ventes du Parc Giron (Giron Park public sales hall) auction every Wednesday afternoon at 2 p.m. Inspection and buyer registration take place during the morning of the sale. In addition, there are four Sunday sales a year of high-quality antiques. Sales and information from Dominique Lemaitre, Parc Giron, allée Drouot, 42100 Saint-Ètienne, telephone 77.32.53.12.

Hôtel des Ventes de la Terrasse (Terrace public sales hall) auction every Tuesday afternoon at 2 p.m. and four special auctions per year of high-quality antiques on Monday and Tuesday evenings. This sales hall is on the north side of the city. Sales and information from M. Denis Ballot, 7 rue Léon Lamaizière, 42000 Saint-Ètienne, telephone 77.93.42.76.

Saint-Flour 15100

Salon d'antiquaires (antique dealers' salon) in mid-August. This is a small fair in the centre of France. For exact dates and more information, contact the Office de Tourisme, 2 place d'Armes, 15100 Cantal, telephone 71.60.22.50.

Saint-Fons 69190

(Please also see Lyon.)

Marché aux puces (flea market) every Sunday morning year round beginning about 6 a.m. until noon on boulevard Sampaix. The market here, part of a general food and miscellaneous merchandise market, is refreshing after near-by Lyons' monstrous and crowded markets. The selection is much smaller—don't plan to find lots of antiques here. Organised by the Service des Marchés, Ville de Saint-Fons, Boîte Postale 100, 69195 Saint-Fons Cedex, telephone 78.70.94.70.

Saint-Georges-les-Baillargeaux 86130

Marché à la brocante (junk market) first Saturday of every month at place de l'Eglise. This small town in west central France offers about two dozen vendors of odds and ends, including old copper and iron pots, wood and iron farm implements, and sometimes traditional pottery.

Saint-Germain-en-Laye 78100

Salle des Ventes (public sales hall) auction every Wednesday at 10 a.m. and 2 p.m. and every Sunday at 2 p.m. This Parisian suburb has a fine selection at close to Parisian prices. Expect high finish and elegance rather than rustic country items. Information and sale site is Salle des Ventes, 13 rue Thiers, 78100 Saint-Germain-en-Laye, telephone 39.73.95.64.

Salon des antiquaires (antique dealers' salon) the end of April to beginning of May (changes yearly) at the Manège Royal. This relatively small show is close to Paris; selection and prices are also similar. Information from Expotrolles-Margeridon, 171 rue du Faubourg Saint-Antoine, 75011 Paris, telephone 43.47.38.00.

Saint-Girons 09200

Foire aux antiquités et à la brocante (antique and junk dealers' fair) second week of August in the town centre, on the August 15 holiday. This is the major annual event of the region, and in addition to the antiques, there are exhibitions of paintings, ancient and modern maps, and gourmet specialities. Information from Foire aux An-

tiquités de Saint-Girons, Boîte Postale 30, 09200
Saint-Girons, telephone 61.66.04.00.

Saint-Malo 35400

Marché à la brocante (junk market) first Friday
of every month near the market hall in the ancient walled city centre. Information from the Office de Tourisme, esplanade Saint-Vincent, 35400
Saint-Malo, telephone 99.86.64.48.

Saint-Ouen-L'Aumone 95310

(Please also see Paris.)

Expositon d'antiquités (antiques exposition)
third weekend of November at the Salle des
Fétes. This is a relatively new fair near Paris.
Organised by the Groupement des Antiquaires
du Vexin-Val d'Oise, 12 rue de Jaigny, 95160
Montmorency, telephone 39.60.04.56.

Saint-Tropez 83990

Marché aux puces (flea market) every Tuesday
and Saturday morning about 8 a.m. on the place
des Lices in this elegant resort village. The antiques and junk are mixed in with the vegetables
and souvenirs; because of the large extent of the
tourist trade, don't expect to make great finds at
this market. Information from Mme. Yolaine
Hery, Syndicat d'Initiative de Bormes, rue Jean
Aicard, 83230 Bormes-les-Mimosas, telephone
94.71.15.17.

Salon des antiquaires (antique dealers' salon)
last Thursday of August to the second Sunday in
September from 10 a.m. to 1 p.m. and 4.30 to
7.30 p.m. at the place des Lices. More than 100
dealers offer antiques and genuine items only.
This is a good show, where you can find
Provençal furniture and minor paintings,
glassware, and occasional wood carvings. The
first day (Thursday) is reserved for dealers only:
have a business card and maybe a copy of a busi-

ness licence ready. For information, contact M. Dominik Julien, Office Culturel et d'Animation de Saint-Tropez, 13 place des Lices, 83990 Saint-Tropez, telephone 94.97.00.13.

Saint-Soupplets 77165

Marché aux puces (flea market) last Sunday of every month except December in the town centre.

Samatan 32130

Salon des antiquaires (antique dealers' salon) fourth weekend and following Monday of August at place de la Mairie in the village centre. This is a major regional fair, with about 70 vendors. (Dealers' day is on Friday—bring some business cards or copy of your business licence and you're in.) Organised by the Association des Commerçants et Artisans de Samatan, Axe Toulouse-Lombez, place de la Mairie, 32130 Samatan, telephone 62.62.31.58.

Samoise-sur-Seine 77920

(Please also see Ferté-Alais, Fontainebleau, and Seine-Port.)

Marché de brocante (junk market) last Sunday of every month except December. This is a relatively small market in the distant outskirts of Paris near Fontainebleau, with about 50 vendors. The market is much larger the last weekend of June, when the market moves onto the island, and about 70 dealers display their wares. Reproductions are prohibited at the June fair. Information from Association de Brocanteurs de Seine et Marne (ABSEM), 100 rue Général de Gaulle, 77780 Bourron-Marlotte, telephone 60.17.14.95.

Savigny-sur-Orge 91600

Marché aux puces (flea market) first Saturday of the month year round at place Davoult and second Saturday of the month as part of the market at the adjoining Marché du Plateau.

Seine-Port 77113

Petit marché aux puces (little flea market) first Sunday of every month except January and September at the place des Tilleuls. This market is close enough to Paris to be influenced by Parisian styles and also prices. Fewer than 50 vendors offer all kinds of odds and ends.

Semur-en-Auxois 21140

Salle des Ventes (public auction house) auction every Sunday at 2 p.m. Inspection and buyer registration take place before the sale begins. Information and sale at the Salle des Ventes, 18 rue du Rempart, 21140 Semur-en-Auxois, telephone 80.97.20.90.

Seyne 83500

(Please see La Seyne 83500.)

Soisy-sous-Montmorency 95230

Marché aux puces (flea market) Wednesday, Saturday, and Sunday year round on avenue de la Division Leclerc. This market, far enough out from Paris to be away from its direct influence, is part antiques and used goods, but even more a food and new merchandise market.

Soumolou 64420

(Please also see Pau.)

Marché aux puces (flea market) first Sunday of the month year round in the town centre. This is one of the small regional markets along the base of the Pyrenees in southern France.

Strasbourg 67000

(Please also see Benfeld.)

Marché aux puces (flea market) Wednesday and Saturday year round from about 7.30 a.m. at the place de l'Viel Hôpital. This picturesque district in one of France's most graceful cities provides a wonderful setting to find old stoneware crocks and butter churns, but only a small amount of solid silver, glasses and wine carafes, and porcelains. Because Strasbourg was part of Germany from 1871 to 1918, be familiar with German hallmarks and expect to see some German porcelains. While the general price level is higher than in much of France, it is lower than nearby Germany for pieces of equivalent quality. Parking is almost impossible in this neighbourhood; you'll have to park across the river. Information from the Service Municipal de Droits de place, Hôtel de Ville, Boîte Postale 1049-1050F, 67070 Strasbourg Cedex, telephone 88.60.90.90, telex C.U.S. 809728 F, fax 88.60.91.00.

Carrefour européen de l'antiquité (European antiques crossroads) show in mid January in Hall 20 at the Parc des Expositions du Wacken. This is a major regional antique show and sale, though there are foreign exhibitors and buyers, particularly from nearby Germany. Organised by Prom'Art, 4 rue Offenbach, 35100 Rennes, telephone 99. 50.74.19, or the local representative, M. Chenkier, 10-12 rue des Dentelles, 67000 Strasbourg, telephone 88.32.82.76.

Tarbes 65000

Marché à la brocante (junk market) first Saturday of every month year round beginning about 8.30 a.m. to late afternoon at the Halle Marcadieu at place Marcadieu in the centre of town. This is a large regional market; local specialities sometimes found include wood carvings, old jewellery and clocks, milk jugs, boxes, and spoons. Information from the Syndicat d'-Initiative, place de Verdun, 65000 Tarbes, telephone 62.93.36.62.

Marché aux puces (flea market) every Thursday from early morning to noon at place Marcadieu as part of the food and general merchandise market. Information from the Syndicat d'-Initiative, place de Verdun, 65000 Tarbes, telephone 62.93.36.62.

Teich 33470

Salon des antiquaires du bassin d'Arcachon (Arcachon basin antique dealers' salon) the week of Bastille Day (July 14) throughout this suburb's centre in the vicinity of Bordeaux. About 50 exhibitors show regional antiques. Information from the Mairie du Teich, 33470 Teich, telephone 56.22.88.09.

Thionville 57100

Marché aux puces (flea market) second and fourth Saturday of every month year round from 6 a.m. to noon between the place de la Liberté and adjoining place de la Liberté, in the centre of town. This relatively large market is one of the older ones. You may occasionally find interesting glass, faïence, stamps, clothes, books, and occasionally small silver and silver plate items. Information from the Office de Tourisme, 16 rue Vieux Collège, 57100 Thionville, telephone 82.53.33.18 or 82.54.40.16.

Salon des antiquaires (antique dealers' salon) the first weekend of October at the Salle Jean Burger, near the theatre in the town centre. This is a good local fair, and reproductions are prohibited. Organised by the Syndicat des Antiquaires de Lorraine, Lichon 57420. Information from the Office de Tourisme, 16 rue Vieux Collège, 57100 Thionville, telephone 82.53.33.18 or 82.54.40.16.

Marché de noël (Christmas market) the second weekend of December at the Centre Jacques Brel at place de la Gare. Antiques and collectables are mixed in with food, toys, and other types of goods. Information from the Office de Tourisme, 16 rue Vieux Collège, 57100 Thionville, telephone 82.53.33.18 or 82.54.40.16.

Thiviers 24800

Marché aux puces (flea market) the weekend closest to Bastille Day (July 14) and also the weekend closest to the 10th of August in the Parc Municipal of this small town in Périgord. These are fine long-established rural markets, with a sprinkling of folk art among the other items. Though few American or Canadian tourists frequent this part of France, this is prime tourist country for the French and other Europeans. Information from the Syndicat d'Initiative, place du Maréchal Foch, Boîte Postale 41, 24800 Thiviers, telephone 53.55.12.50.

Thouars 79100

Foire des antiquités et de la brocante (antique and junk fair) second Friday through following Monday of April at square Franklin Roosevelt. This regional country fair in a quiet country town is enjoyable; exhibitors bring regional items such as glass, wood carvings, faience, and clocks. Organised by the Comité de la Foire du 15 avril, Mairie du Thouars, Boîte 183, 79103 Thouars Cedex, telephone 49.68.11.11.

Toulon 83100

Marché aux puces (flea market) every Sunday morning in the Quartier Sainte-Musse at the Parc des Expositons. This market is on the eastern side of the city, in the area of the sports arena and not far from the Gare Maritime. This market attracts about 250 to 300 vendors. You may find some items of Algerian origin, as well as quantities of maritime and fishing gear. Finds can be made at this market, in part because the region is economically depressed and is far off the usual tourist paths. Organised by the 4e Division, Service des Emplacements, Ville de Toulon, Hôtel de Ville, Boîte Postale 1407, 83056 Toulon Cedex, telephone 94.92.73.37.

Salon international indépendant de l'antiquité (international independent antique salon) at the Parc des Expositions in July, centred on Bastille Day (July 14). This is a relatively small regional fair. Information from Var Expansion, Parc des Expositions de Sainte-Musse, 83058 Toulon.

Toulouse 31000

Marché aux puces (flea market) Saturday and Monday from 8 a.m. to 6 p.m. and Sunday from 8 a.m. to noon, in place Saint-Sernin, facing Basilique Saint-Sernin. This is a large market in a lively city; specialities you may find here include turn-of-the century art work of all types, including bronze statues, paintings, and sculpture; brass door knobs, door knockers, and hinges; and late 19th-century glassware. Organised by the Ville de Toulouse, Mairie, Direction des Droits de Stationnement, 30148 Toulouse Cedex, telephone 61.22.23.72.

Brocante de printemps (spring junk fair) from the first Wednesday to the following Sunday of March at the Parc des Expositions, in the park on the island in the middle of the Garonne river. This is a major market, with about 150 vendors, who are mostly full-time dealers. Organised by Sforman S. A., 31 rue du Rempart-Matabiau, 31000 Toulouse, telephone 61.21.93.25 or 61.21.81.26.

Salon des antiquaires de Languedoc-Midi-Pyrénées (Languedoc-Midi-and Pyrenees antique dealers' salon) first Thursday to second Sunday of November at the Parc des Expositions, on the island in the Garonne river. This is one of the major antique fairs of France: over 350 dealers from many areas of France sell their wares. Only true antiques may be sold. Experts and appraisers are available. The two days before fair is open to the pubilc are reserved for members of the antiques trade; bring a business card or copy of a business licence. An admission charge is collected from the public. Organised by Sforman S. A., 31 rue du Rempart-Matabiau, 31000 Toulouse, telephone 61.21.93.25 or 61.21.81.26.

Tournus 71700

Salon des antiquaires (antique dealers' salon) fourth Sunday of May until the first Sunday of June in the beautiful, historic and well-preserved district around the Romanesque Abbey of Saint-Philibert. This is a good sized regional sale, where you may find all types of old items, and pieces of ancient and old Burgundian walnut furniture. Information from the Office de Tourisme, place Carnot, 71700 Tournus, telephone 85.51.13.10, or the organiser, U.C.I.A., Boîte Postale 20, 71700 Tournus, telephone 85.51.06.03.

Tours 37000

Marché aux puces (flea market) Wednesday and Saturday mornings year round at place de la Victoire, near the food market on the western side of the old city centre. The market has depth, but there are few local specialty items aside from faïence. This area is full of junk shops with broken-down furniture and gold 19th-century items. Organised by the Service des Places, Ville de Tours, Hôtel de Ville, Place Jean Jaurés, 37000 Tours. Information from the Office de Tourisme, place du Maréchal Leclerc, 37042 Tours Cedex, telephone 47.05.58.08, telex 750008 F.

Salon des antiquaires (antique dealers' salon) in mid-March. This large regional show moves from place to place in the city, but is sometimes held at the Parc des Expositions along the River Cher: contact the organisers for details. Information from Prom'Art, 11 impasse Beethoven, 35100 Rennes, telephone 99.50.74.19.

Salon Tourangeau de l'objet de collection (Tours salon of the collectable object) the third weekend of October at the Parc des Expositions, near the Autoroute crossing of the River Cher. Organised by M. Mouton, 27 rue Brémond d'Ars, 29130 Quimperlé, telephone 98.39.02.00.

Puces Tourangelles (Tours flea market) the weekend of All Saints' Day (November 1) along the river. This is one of the larger weekend markets in the Loire Valley. Information from Prom'Art, 11 impasse Beethoven, 35100 Rennes, telephone 99.50.74.19.

Trouville-sur-Mer 14360

Salons des antiquaires (antique dealers' salons) twice a year for 10 days, beginning May 1 and November 1 at the casino. This is an elegant small show at a classic summer resort along the Atlantic shore. Information from the organisers at the Casino de Trouville, place du Maréchal Foch, 14360 Trouville-sur-Mer, telephone 31.88.76.09.

Troyes 10000

Marché aux puces (flea market) Saturday morning at place Saint Rémy, and adjoining rue Passerat. This vibrant market in an untouristed but picturesque city is interesting. There are finds to be made, especially in heavy provincial furniture, wood and stone carvings, and rustic pictures. This market is part of the regular Saturday food and general market. Information from the Office de Tourisme, 16 boulevard Carnot, Boîte Postale 4082, 10014 Troyes Cédex, telephone 25.73.00.36, telex 8400216 F OKTROY.

Marché de la brocante (junk market) third Sunday of every month year round from 8 a.m. to 7 p.m. at the place de la Cathédrale in the city centre. This market is strictly for antiques and junk but no new items or food. Information from the Office de Tourisme, 16 boulevard Carnot, Boîte Postale 4082, 10014 Troyes Cédex, telephone 25.73.00.36, telex 8400216 F OKTROY.

Salon des antiquaires (antique dealers' salon) the first weekend of May (starting on Friday) every year at the Parc des Expositions on the boulevard de Belgique. This is the major antiques event of the region, with dozens of dealers and some on-site expert appraisers. Free parking is available in a large car park across the street. Information is available from M. Robert Richard, Route Sens-Troyes, Le Mineroy, 10160 Aix-en-Othe, telephone 25.46.72.69.

Les puces d'octobre (October flea market) the last weekend of October at the Parc des Expositions on the boulevard de Belgique. This is one of the largest markets in the region, with hundreds of vendors. Free parking is available in a large car park across the street. Information from the Office de Tourisme, 16 boulevard Carnot, Boôte Postale 4082, 10014 Troyes Cédex, telephone 25.73.00.36, telex 8400216 F OKTROY.

Tulle 19000

Salon des antiquités et de la brocante (antique and junk salon) Easter Sunday and the following Monday at the Centre Culturel et Sportif, 36 avenue Alsace-Lorraine, near the railway station. This minor regional fair in a poor region of France is interesting for the ambience, and you may find occasional pieces of folk art. Organised by Mme. Thoumieux, 14 rue Gondinet, 87000 Limoges, telephone 52.32.15.61. Information from the Secrétaire, Office de Tourisme, quai Baluze, 19000 Tulle, telephone 55.26.59.61.

Ury 77116

Dépot d'antiquités et brocante le Cheval Blanc (White Horse antique and junk depot) every Friday, Saturday, Sunday and Monday from 10 a.m. to 7 p.m. (only afternoon on Friday and Monday) about 10 kilometres south of Fontainebleau (take Autoroute A6, exit at Route Nationale 152, and follow R.N. 152 to the intersection of D.63). This is not a market but rather a warehouse full of antiques and collectables. Parking is available, but this location cannot be reached on public transport. Organised by M. Arlette Paillard-Savidan, 1 rue de Fontainebleau, 77116 Ury, telephone 64.24.44.47.

Valence 26000

Marché aux puces (flea market) first Sunday morning of every month at place Saint-Jean, in and around the market hall. Information from the Régies Communales, Mairie de Valence, place de la Liberté, Boîte Postale 2119, 26021 Valence Cédex, telephone 75.43.93.00.

Salon des antiquaires et brocanteurs (antique and junk dealers' salon) third weekend of November at the Palais de la Foire. This fair is especially strong in antique cars and old automotive items. Information from the Office de Tourisme, place Général Leclerc, 26000 Valence, telephone 75.43.04.88, telex 345265 F, or from the organiser, M. Bruno, Boîte Postale 703, 26007 Valence Cédex, telephone 75.90.01.76.

Vannes 56000

Marché aux puces (flea market) first Saturday of the month year round from 8 a.m. to 4 p.m. around and in front of the church of Saint-Patern about 100 metres outside the city gate. Information from the Office de Tourisme, 1 rue Thiers, 56000 Vannes, telephone 97.47.24.34.

Salon des antiquaires du pay Vannetais (Vannes region antique dealers' salon) the weekend of All Saints' Day (November 1) at the place de la Cathédrale in the town centre. This is a local fair. Organised by M. A. Guillou, 56 Grandchamp, 56000 Vannes, telephone 97.66.78.78.

Hôtel des Ventes (public sales hall) auction every Saturday year round at 2 p.m. This auction often has old Breton furniture, and jewellery and wood carvings. Information and buyer registration is held Friday from 9 a.m. to noon, and from 2 to 6.30 p.m., and Saturday morning. Information and sale location is Hôtel des Ventes de Vannes, 9 rue Saint-Guenhaël (in the town centre), Boîte Postale 37, 56001 Vannes Cédex, telephone 97.47.26.82.

Vatan 36150

Foire à la brocante (junk fair) fourth Sunday of September (starts early!) on the rue des Récollets. This minor market in a small village in the centre of France is small, but may be worthwhile if you're already in the area. Organised by M. Pourchasse, 24 rue F. Charbonnier, 36150 Vatan, telephone 54.49.70.86.

Vence 06140

Marché à la brocante (junk market) every Wednesday in the Parking de Lara in this Riviera town. Information from the Offece de Touirsme, place Grand-Jardin, 06140 Vence, telephone 93.58.06.38.

Vendôme 41100

Petit marché aux puces (small flea market) Friday as part of the general market. Only about half a dozen vendors offer a miscellany of junk and second-hand items; the rest of the market is given over to food, clothes, tools, etc. The first weekend of September, there are about 40 dealers offering junk and other odds and ends. Information from the Office de Tourisme, rue Poterie, Boîte Postale 34, 41101 Vendôme Cédex, telephone 54.77.05.07.

Marché aux puces (flea market) in the quartier des Rottes. This market, with used goods and a few antiques mixed in with new goods and food vendors, is animated and picturesque. Information from the Office de Tourisme, rue Poterie,

Boîte Postale 34, 41101 Vendôme Cédex, telephone 54.77.05.07.

Braderie, foire à la brocante et petit marché aux puce (braderie, junk fair, and small flea market) first Saturday of September in the town centre. This is the largest market of the year in the area, and is one that almost resembles a boot sale, with hundreds of non-commercial vendors selling all types of goods. Organised by the Union Commerciale et Artisanale du Vendomois (U.C.A.V.), 7 place de la République, 41100 Vendîme, telephone 54.77.05.73.

Verdun 55100

Salle des Ventes (public sales hall) auction every Saturday at 2 p.m. Sometimes beautiful Lorrain oak furniture, art nouveau, art deco, faïence, chairs, jewellery, and other old or antique items are on the auction block. Inspection and buyer registration takes place before the sale. Information from M. Eric Hertz at Salle des Ventes, 1 place de la Gare, 55100 Verdun, telephone 29.86.24.67.

Foire aux antiquités (antique fair) in mid-February at the Salle Palyvalente in the Cité Anthouard district. At this well-established regional fair, you're likely to find jewellery, paintings, typical Lorraine furniture, and souvenirs and weapons from the World War I battle fought on the ridge just east of town. Information from M. Lucien Baugnon, Chemin de Cendrousse, 55100 Verdun, telephone 29.86.23.69, fax 29.84.56.03.

Versailles 78000

(Please also see Chatou and Paris.)

Petit marché aux puces (little flea market) every Saturday and Sunday from 9.30 a.m. until 7 p.m. on passage de la Geôle, behind the Eglise Notre-Dame in the angle of boulevard de la Reine and rue Rameau. This passage has outdoor vendors as well as regular merchants indoors. You'll find minor jewellery, arms, books, and occasional Oriental pieces. Information from Passage et Cour des Antiquaires, 10 rue Rameau, 78000 Versailles, telephone 39.53.84.96.

Salon des antiquaires (antique dealers' salon) at beginning of June, at the Orangerie of the Chateau. This salon attempts to recreate the great century of Versailles: rather nice pieces are shown here (at rather high prices). Organised by S. O. P. A., 14 Route de Nantes, 44650 Legé.

Biennale les antiquaires au château (biennial antique dealers at the chateau) the last weekend of September to the second Sunday of October of odd numbered years at the Orangerie of the Chateau. Organzed by M. Philippe Boucaud, 25 rue du Bac, 75007 Paris, telephone 42.61.24.07.

Salle des Ventes (public sales hall) auctions every Sunday at 2 p.m. and every Wednesday at 9.30 a.m. Inspection and buyer registration is held before the sales begin. Information and sales from Salle des Ventes, 3 impasse des Chevau Légers, 78000 Versailles, telephone 39.50.75.04.

Vervins 02140

Salle des Ventes (public sales hall) auction Wednesday and Fridays from 2.30 p.m. to 7 p.m. and Saturday from 10 a.m. to noon. Inspection of items to be sold and buyer registration is held before the sale begins. Information and sales at the Salle des Ventes, 8 rue de la Republique, 02140 Vervins.

Villefranche-du-Périgord 24550

Foire à la brocante (junk fair) the weekend following August 15 throughout this small, picturesque town. It is to some degree a tourist attraction, but the fair has some rustic furniture and farm items from about 60 vendors, mostly dealers. There is no admission fee. An authorized expert is on the fair site, who will assess antiques and informally appraise items for no charge. Information from the M. Issard, Syndicat d'Initiative, Mairie, 24550 Villefranche-du-Périgord, telephone 53.29.91.44.

Villeneuve-les-Avignon 30400

(Please also see Avignon.)

Salon des antiquaires (antique dealers' salon) first Friday to second Sunday of September at the Chartreuse de Val de Bénédiction. This major regional elegant show is vetted; only dealers may exhibit and only antiques may be sold. No reproductions are permitted. Information from M. Michel Joubert, Mairie de Villeneuve-les-Avignon, 30400 Villeneuve-les-Avignon, telephone 90.25.42.03.

Vire 14500

Hôtel des Ventes (public sales hall) every Saturday at 2.30 p.m. and occasionally on Sundays as well. Inspection and buyer registration is before the sale begins. Information from the Hôtel des Ventes, 4 rue du Cotin, 14500 Vire, telephone 31.68.17.19.

Vitry-le-François 51300

Salle des Ventes (public sales hall) auction every Saturday at 2 p.m., and at least three special Sunday auctions per year of old tools, antiques, and folk art. Inspection of merchandise and buyer registration is held on Saturday morning from 9 to 11 a.m. Catalogues are issued for some auctions. Information and catalogues from the Salle des Ventes, 9 Faubourg Léon-Bourgeois, 51300 Vitry-le-François, telephone 26.74.75.02.

Vittel 88800

Salon vosgien des antiquaires (Vosges region antique dealers' salon) Friday to Monday at Pentecost (the fifth Sunday after Easter—often in May) at the Palais de Congrès. This is one of the largest regional fairs in Lorraine; dealers show only original items such as furniture, glassware, crystal, and copper. Reproductions are strictly forbidden. Appraisers are on duty.

This turn-of-the-century thermal resort has clearly seen better days, but to visit Vittel is to see an engaging snapshot of earlier times. Information from Mme. Jackie Français, Syndicat des Antiquaires et Brocanteurs des Vosges, 180 rue Division Leclerc, 88800 Vittel, telephone 29.08.47.91 and 29.08.04.67.

Xaronval (Charmes) 88130

Foire vosgienne de brocante à Xaronval (Vosges junk fair at Xaronval) the last weekend of September, near the village of Charmes. This is a regional fair with perhaps 50 dealers trying to sell their items. Information from M. Maurice Lacourt, 6 rue du Général Marion, Xaronval, 88130 Charmes, telephone 29.38.12.41.

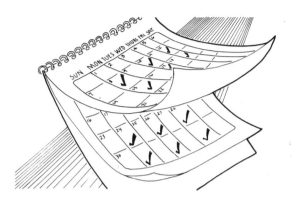

Calendar of Fairs and Markets

Many major antiques trade events take place once or twice a year, a few once every two years.

The brief listing below is merely a calendar, divided by month, and within each month alphabetically. Complete details for each event below are found in the alphabetical city in the book. You may wish to plan your journey to coincide with these major fairs and shows.

Be sure to contact the organiser to confirm that the time and venue have not been changed.

January

Bordeaux: Salon des antiquaires de Bordeaux-Laînè, mid January.

Enghien-les-Bains: Foire d'antiquités et brocante, mid January.

Grenoble: Salon Européen des antiquaires, end of January and beginning of February.

Nogent-sur-Marne, Salon des antiquaires, third weekend of January.

Rennes: Marché aux puces Rennaises, last week of January.

Strasbourg: Carrefour européen de l'antiquité, mid January.

February

Avignon: Salon des antiquaires, second week of February.

Avignon: Marché d'un jour reservés aux professionels, mid February.

Bordeaux: Salon des antiquaires Bordeaux-Lac, second week of February.

Bourges: Journées de l'antiquité, second weekend of February.

Draguignan: Salon d'antiquités et brocante du Var, first weekend of February.

Montpellier: Foire aux anes, first Monday of February.

Paris: Foire internationale à la brocante et de l'antiquité, last week of February.

Pau: Salon des antiquaires, mid February.

Verdun: Foire aux antiquités, mid February.

March

Brest: Foire à la brocante, first weekend of March.

Chatou (near Paris): Foire nationale à la brocante, beginning of March.

Milly-le-Forêt: Foire à la brocante, second weekend of March.

Orléans: Salon des antiquaires et de la brocante, second week of March.

Toulouse: Brocante de printemps, first Wednesday to following Sunday of March.

Tours: Salon des antiquaires, mid March.

April

Aigle: Salon des antiquaires et brocanteurs, Easter weekend.

Angers: Broc et puces, last weekend of April.

Antibes: Salon des antiquaires, two weeks around Easter.

Barjac: Foire de Barjac, Easter Sunday and following Monday.

Bernay: Salon des antiquaires, Easter weekend.

Champagne-sur-Oise, Salon d'antiquaires et brocanteurs, first weekend of April.

Crozon: Foire à la brocante, first week of April.

Epinal: Foire de printemps de l'antiquité, Easter weekend.

Fontainebleau: Journées nationales de la brocante, mid-April.

Fontainebleau: Biennale de Fontainebleau, end of April to beginning of May of odd numbered years.

Le Mans: 24 heures de la brocante, second weekend of April.

L'Isle-sur-Sorgue: Foire à brocante, Easter week and the Monday after Easter.

Liseaux: Salon de l'objet ancienne et multi- collections, end of April.

Mauvezin: Foire à la brocante, beginning of April.

Montpellier: Salon des antiquaires et de la brocante, 25th of April to second Sunday of May.

Nancy: Salon des antiquités, mid April.

Nolay: Foire à la brocante et aux antiquités, Easter Sunday and Monday.

Orange: Grande brocante d'Orange, Easter weekend.

Périgueux: Salon des antiquaires, Easter weekend.

Perpignan: Salon des antiquaires du Roussillon, around Easter week.

Rouen: Salon des antiquaires de la Halle aux Toiles, end of April and beginning of May.

Saint-Germaine-en-Laye: Salon des antiquaires, end of April and beginning of May.

Thouars: Foire des antiquités et de la brocante, second Friday to following Monday of April.

Tulle: Salon des antiquités, Easter Sunday and following Monday.

May

Aumale: Foire à la brocante, third Sunday of May.

Chambéry: Salon des antiquaires et brocanteurs, mid-May.

Colmar: Salon des antiquaires, first or second week of May.

Dijon: Salon des antiquaires et de la brocante, two weeks in May.

Etampes: Salon des antiquaires, Ascension weekend.

L'Isle-sur-la-Sorgue: Foire à la brocante, Pentecost.

Eauze: Salon des antiquaires, first half of May.

Meyrargues: Foire des brocanteurs, end of May or beginning of June.

Obernai: Foire à la brocante, second week of May.

Poitiers: Foire à la brocante, Pentecost Sunday and the following Monday.

Tournus: Salon des antiquaires, fourth Sunday of May to first Sunday of June.

Trouville-sur-Mer: Salon des antiquaires, May 1 to May 10.

Troyes: Salon des antiquaires, first weekend of May.

Vittel: Salon Vosgien des antiquaires, Friday to Sunday at Pentecost (usually in May).

June

Aigues-Mortes: Foire à la brocante, third weekend of June.

Belfort: Salon aux antiquités, third week of June.

Caen: Salon des antiquaires, second weekend to third weekend of June.

Magny-en-Vexin: Salon d'antiquités et brocante, mid-June.

Rouen: Foire à la ferraille, fourth Sunday and Monday of June.

Versailles: Salon des antiquaires, beginning of June.

July

Amboise: Salon d'antiquités, firsthalf of July.

Apt: Foire à la brocante, last weekend of July to following Tuesday.

Chinon, Salon des antiquaires et de la brocante, third weekend of July.

Cusset: Salon des antiquaires et de la brocante, second week of July.

Mirande: Salon des antiquaires, week of Bastille Day (July 14).

Mouans-Sartoux: Foire à la brocante, third weekend of July.

Narbonne: Foire à la brocante, first half of July.

Pont Saint-Esprit: Foire des antiquités et brocante, first weekend of July.

Teich: Salon des antiquaires du bassin d'-Arcachon, week of Bastille Day (July 14).

Thiviers: Marché aux puces, weekend closest to Bastille Day (July 14).

Toulon: Salon international indépendant de l'antiquité, week of Bastille Day (July 14).

August

Annecy: Salon d'antiquités de la rentrée, end of August.

Barjac: Foire de Barjac, Assumption Day holiday (August 15 and adjoining days).

Cabourg: Foire d'antiquités, week of August 15.

Chartres: Journées brocantes et antiquités, Ascension wekend.

Crèvecour-le-Grande, Marché aux puces, second Thursday of August.

Divonne-les-Bains: Grande foire aux antiquaires et brocanteurs, third weekend of August.

Fayence: Foire de la brocante, first weekend of August.

Gien: Foire des antiquités et brocante, fourth weekend of August.

Joyeuse: Foire à la brocante, weekend after August 15.

L'Isle-sur-Sorgue: Foire à la brocante, Assumption Day (August 15) weekend.

Nolay: Foire à la brocante et aux antiquaires, Assumption Day weekend.

Orange: Grande brocante d'Orange, Assumption Day weekend.

Pornic: Brocante et curiosités, first Sunday of August.

Remiremont: Foire brocante champêtre, first weekend of August.

Saint-Flour: Salon d'antiquaires, mid-August.

Saint-Girons: Foire aux antiquités et à la brocante, second week of August.

Saint-Tropez: Salon des antiquaires, last Thursday of August to second Sunday in September.

Samatan: Salon des antiquaires, fourth weekend of August and the following Monday.

Thiviers: Marché aux puces, second weekend of August.

Villefranche-du-Périgord: Foire à la brocante, last weekend of August.

September

Aigle: Salon des antiquaires et brocanteurs, third weekend of September.

Aix-en-Provence: Salon des antiquaires, second half of September.

Arles: Salon des antiquaires et de la brocante, last week of September.

Arles: Salon des antiquités et de la brocante, last week of September.

Auch: Salon des antiquaires, first 15 days of September.

Avignon: Foire à la brocante, beginning of September.

Bar-le-Duc: Salon des antiquaires, second week of September.

Bourg-en-Bresse: Salon des antiquaires, second and third weeks of September.

Charmes: La Foire Vosgienne des brocanteurs, last weekend of September.

Chatou (near Paris): Foire nationale à la brocante, end of September.

Compiègne: Salon des antiquaires, second Thursday to following Sunday of September.

Durtal: Grande rendez-vous de la brocante, last Sunday in September.

Lille: Grande braderie, first Monday after the first Sunday of September.

Maisons-Laffitte: Exposition d'antiquaires, in September.

Metz: Foire des brocanteurs, second Sunday of September.

Moret-sur-Loing: Foire à la brocante, first weekend of September.

Paris: Biennale internationale des antiquaires, third week of September to second Sunday of October of even-numbered years.

Paris—Ivry-sur-Seine: Internationale de l'antiquité et à la brocante, last week of September.

Rennes: Salon des antiquaires, last weekend of September.

Vatan: Foire à la brocante, fourth Sunday of September.

Vendôme: Braderie, foire à la brocante et petit marchéaux puces, first Saturday of September.

Villeneuve-les-Avignon: Salon des antiquaires, first Friday to second Sunday of September.

Xaronval: Foire vosgienne de brocante, last weekend of September.

October

Aix-les-Bains: Exposition-vente d'antiquités, early October.

Albi: Foire à la brocante et aux antiquaires, first weekend in October.

Alençon: Salon d'automne d'antiquités et de la brocante, end of October.

Auch: Salon des antiquaires et floralies, third week of October.

Aumale: Foire à la brocante, third Sunday of October.

Auxerre: Salon des antiquaires, mid-October.

Besançon: Salon Comptoise des antiquaires, first week of October.

Blois: Salon des antiquaires, third week of October.

Douai: Braderie-brocante, first Sunday of October.

Guingamp: Foire à la brocante, fourth weekend of October.

Lamorlaye: Exposition d'antiquaires, beginning of October.

Lille: Salon de l'antiquité: second weekend of October.

Marseille: Salon des antiquaires, third week of October.

Nogent-le-Rotrou: Salon des antiquaires, beginning of October.

Obernai: Foire à la brocante, October 30 to November 2.

Perpignan: Salon des antiquaires du Roussillon, in October (exact dates vary).

Poitiers: Salon des antiquaires, third weekend of October.

Pontault-Combault: Foire aux antiquités, ssecond weekend of October.

Reims: Salon des antiquaires, second half of October.

Rouen: Salon national des antiquaires, second to third week of October.

Thionville: Salon des antiquaires,first weekend of October.

Tours: Salon Tourangeau de l'objet de collection, third weekend of October.

Troyes: Les puces d'Octobre, last weekend of October.

Versailles: Biennale les antiquaires au château, last weekend of September to second Sunday of October in odd- numbered years.

November

Ferté-Alais, Foire de brocante, first weekend of November.

Fayence: Foire de antiquités et de la brocante, All Saints' weekend (beginning of November).

Givors: Foire à la paperasserie, second weekend of November.

Metz: Salon des antiquaires, second half of November.

Montpellier: Foire aux anes, beginning of November.

Obernai: Foire à la brocante, October 31- November 2.

Pont Saint-Esprit: Salon des antiquités, four-day weekend around Armistice Day (November 11).

Pont-sur-Yonne: Foire aux antiquités, third weekend of November.

Saint-Brieuc, Foire à la brocante, last weekend of November (some years first weekend of December).

Saint-Étienne: Salon en Forez des antiquaires et brocanteurs, beginning of November.

Saint-Ouen-l'Aumone: Exposition d'antiquités, third weekend of November.

Toulouse: Salon des antiquaires de Languedoc-Midi- Pyrénées, first Thursday to following Sunday of November.

Tours: Puces Tourangelles, All Saints Day weekend (November 1).

Trouville-sur-Mer: Salon des antiquaires, November 1 to 10.

Valence: Salon des antiquaires et brocanteurs, third weekend of November.

Vannes: Salon d'antiquaires du pay Vannetais, All Saints Day weekend (November 1).

December

Angoulême: Salon des antiquaires, first weekend of December.

Dourdan: Foire de la brocante, second weekend of December.

Le Mans: Salon d'antiquaires, first week of December.

Mâcon: Foire à la brocante, first weekend of December.

Metz: Marché aux puces de Noël, first Sunday of December.

Montauban: Salon des antiquaires et brocanteurs de Quercy, first Thursday to following Sunday of December.

Nantes: Salon de l'antiquité, third weekend of November.

Nîmes: Salon des antiquaires et brocanteurs, second week of December.

Orléans: Foire à la brocante, mid-December.

Poitiers: Foire à la brocante, second Sunday and Monday of December.

Saint-Brieuc: Foire à la brocante et aux antiquités, first weekend of December.

Thionville: Marché de noël, second weekend of December.

Auctions City by City

Many cities and towns in France have regularly scheduled auctions. Most take place in public sales halls ("Salle des Ventes"). A list of towns and cities with auctions follow, including the usual days and starting time of sales. Viewing is held before the sales begin. Details for each auction is in the alphabetical city listings.

Angers, Tuesday, 2 p.m.

Auxerre, Friday, 2 p.m.

Avignon, Thursday, 9 a.m., and two Sundays per month at 2.30

Bayeux, every Saturday (occasionally Sunday), 2.30 p.m.

Bergerac, Wednesday and Saturday, plus special auctions.

Bernay, some but not all Saturdays and Sundays.

Béziers, irregularly throughout the year.

Bolbec, two Saturdays per month, 2 p.m.

Bordeaux (Hôtel des Ventes), cours du Médoc, Thursday, 2.30 p.m.

Bordeaux, rue de Cheverus, Tuesday, Wednesday, and Thursday, 2 p.m.

Bourg-en-Bresse, irregularly throughout the year.

Brest, Tuesday 2 p.m., Tuesday evenings 7 p.m.

Brive-la-Gaillarde, Saturday, 2 p.m.

Calais, Sunday, 2.30 p.m.

Chalon-sur-Saône, Thursday and Saturday,
2 p.m.

Chartres (Hôtel des Ventes), Tuesday and
Sunday, 2 p.m.

Chateauroux, Thursday, 2 p.m. (closed month
of August).

Chateau-Thierry, first and third Friday of
every month, 2 p.m.

Chinon, Monday, 2.30 p.m.

Deauville, Sunday, 10 a.m. and 2 p.m.

Dieppe, Saturday, 2 p.m.

Dijon, rue de Gray, Wednesday and some
Sundays, 2 p.m.

Dijon, rue Paul Cabet, Thursday, 9.30 a.m. and
2 p.m.

Dijon, rue des Godrans, Friday, 2 p.m.

Duclair, Sunday, 2 p.m.

Enghien-les-Baines, twice a month (call for
dates and times).

Fontainebleau, Friday and Sunday afternoon.

Granville, Saturday or Sunday, 2.30 p.m.

Joigny, Saturday or Sunday (it varies),
    2.30 p.m.

Lacroix-Saint-Ouen, irregularly held (call for
dates and times).

Laon, Saturday, 2.30 p.m.

Lille, rue des Jardins, Saturday 2 p.m.

Lille, rue Saint-Anne, Monday 2 p.m.

Lyon, rue des Tuiliers, Monday and Wednesday, 2 p.m.

Lyon, rue de Cronstadt, twice a week.

Lyon, rue Charles Bienner, at irregular intervals.

Lyon, avenue Sidoine-Appolinaire, at irregular intervals.

Mâcon, Saturday, 2.30 p.m.

Marseille, Wednesday, Friday, and Saturday, 2.30 p.m.

Meaux, Saturday and some Sundays, 2 p.m.

Nantes, Monday, Wednesday, and Friday, 2 p.m.

Nîmes, Monday and Thursday, 9 a.m.

Nogent-le-Rotrou, every Saturday and one Sunday per month, 2 p.m.

Orléans, at irregular intervals.

Paris, Hôtel Drouot, daily except Sunday, 2 p.m.; closed entire month of August.

Paris, Drouot Nord, Monday to Friday, 9 a.m.; closed entire month of August.

Paris, Crédit Municipal de Paris, variable days, 10.30 a.m.

Périgueux, Wednesday, 2 p.m.

Pontoise, every Monday and last Saturday of month, 2.30 p.m.

Saint-Brieuc, Tuesday, 2 p.m.

Saint-Ètienne, Parc Giron, Wednesday, 2 p.m.

Saint-Ètienne, la Terrasse, Tuesday, 2 p.m.

Saint-Germain-en-Laye, Wednesday, 10 a.m. and 2 p.m., and Sunday, 2 p.m.

Semur-en-Auxois, Sunday, 2 p.m.

Vannes (Hôtel des Ventes), Saturday, 2 p.m.

Verdun, Saturday, 2 p.m.

Vervins, Wednesday and Friday, 2.30 p.m., Saturday, 10 a.m.

Vire, Hôtel des Ventes, Saturday, 2.30 p.m.

Vitry-le-François, every Saturday, 2 p.m., plus special Sunday sales

List of Illustrations

183

List of Maps

Maps of France

The map on this page is the key map to the detailed maps on the following pages. Page numbers on this map refer to the following pages.

Each town location listed is mentioned in the text: only locations with at least one flea market, one antiques show or fair, or a public auction hall are shown.

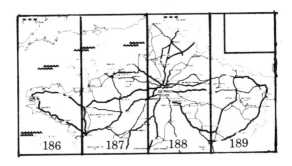

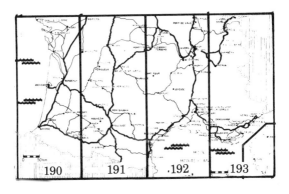

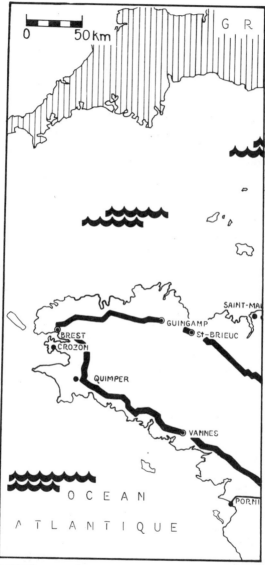

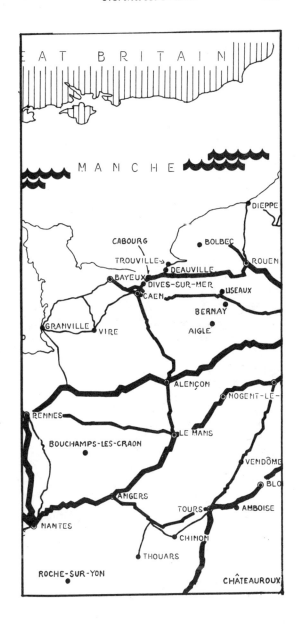

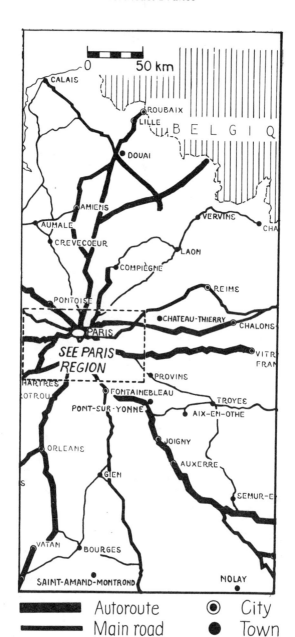

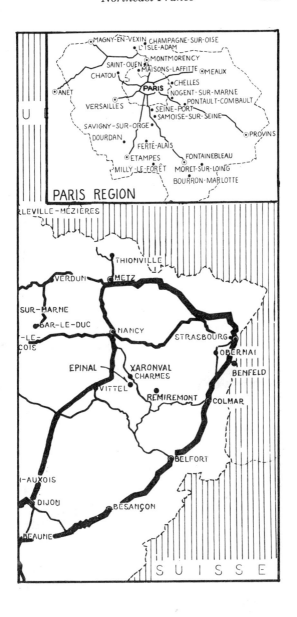

PARIS REGION

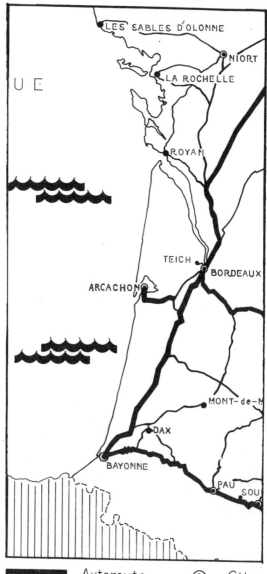

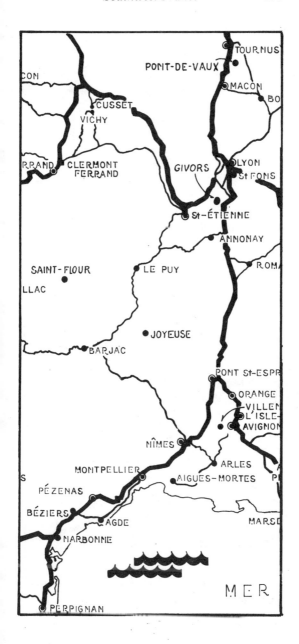

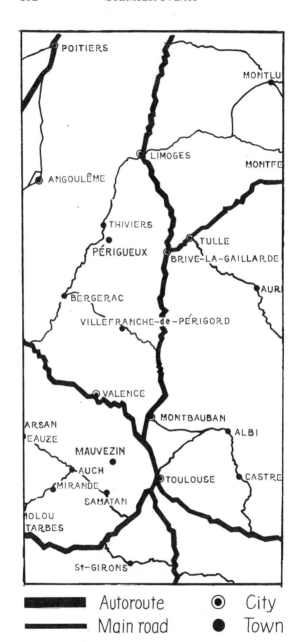

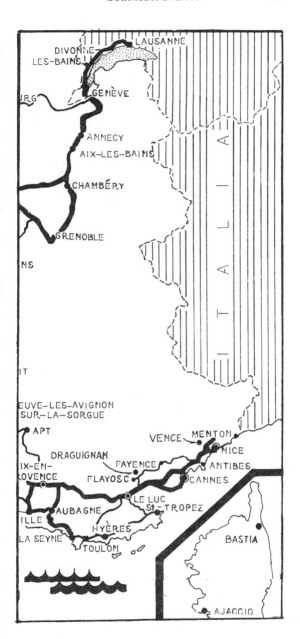

France by Départements

France is divided into administrative regions called "Départements", named after on natural features such as rivers and mountains within each département. A number is assigned to each département. With a few exceptions, numbers are in alphabetical order (for example 01 = Ain, 02 = Aisne, etc.). These numbers are used for everything from car licence numbers to postal codes.

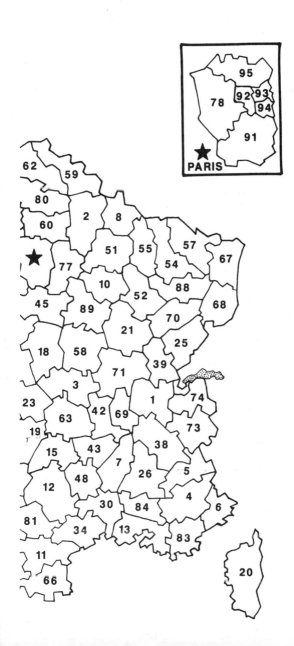

Départements of France

(Keyed to map on previous two pages.)

01 Ain
02 Aisne
03 Allier
04 Alpes-de-Haut-Provence
05 Hautes Alpes
06 Alpes-Maritimes
07 Ardèche
08 Ardennes
09 Ariège
10 Aube
11 Aude
12 Aveyron
13 Bouches-du-Rhône
14 Calvados
15 Cantal
16 Charente
17 Charente-Maritime
18 Cher
19 Corrèze
2A or 20 Corse du Sud (Corsica South)
2B or 20 Haute-Corse (Upper Corsica)
21 Côte-d'Or
22 Côtes-du-Nord
23 Creuse
24 Dordogne
25 Doubs
26 Drôme
27 Eure
28 Eure-et-Loir
29 Finistère
30 Gard
31 Haute Garonne
32 Gers
33 Gironde
34 Hérault
35 Ille-et-Vilaine
36 Indre
37 Indre-et-Loire

38 Isère
39 Jura
40 Landes
41 Loir-et-Cher
42 Loire
43 Loire (Haute)
44 Loire-Atlantique
45 Loiret
46 Lot
47 Lot-et-Garonne
48 Lozère
49 Maine-et-Loire
50 Manche
51 Marne
52 Marne (Haute)
53 Mayenne
54 Meurthe-et-Moselle
55 Meuse
56 Morbihan
57 Moselle
58 Nièvre
59 Nord
60 Oise
61 Orne
62 Pas-de-Calais
63 Puy-de-Dôme
64 Pyrénées-Atlantiques
65 Pyrénées (Hautes)
66 Pyrénées-Orientales
67 Rhin (Bas)
68 Rhin (Haut)
69 Rhône
70 Saône (Haute)
71 Saône-et-Loire
72 Sarthe
73 Savoie
74 Savoie (Haute)
75 Paris
76 Seine-Maritime
77 Seine-et-Marne
78 Yvelines
79 Sàvres (Deux)
80 Somme
81 Tarn

82　Tarn-et-Garonne
83　Var
84　Vaucluse
85　Vendée
86　Vienne
87　Vienne (Haute)
88　Vosges
89　Yonne
90　Belfort (Territoire de)
91　Essonne
92　Hauts-de-Seine
93　Seine-St-Denis
94　Val-de-Marne
95　Val-d'Oise

Index

Will You Help?

Time passes, events change. Almost as soon as this book went to the printer, things changed: some shows moved location, others were cancelled, others increased in size or scope, others gained a focus on a particular type of item. Some flea markets may move because of urban renewal or other reasons.

Won't you please let us know? If you do, we'll be able to improve the next edition of this book. Then, future readers can benefit from your findings.

Either tear out this page, or feel free to use other sheets of paper.

Sincerely,

Peter Manston

What did you find different?

What problems did you find?

Is there any way to avoid this problem?

What markets or fairs moved time or place?

What was your greatest success and most wonderful find?

Thank you very much!

Please send your comments to:

Peter Manston
c/o B.T. Batsford
4 Fitzhardinge Street
London W1H 0AH

Will You Help?

Time passes, events change. Almost as soon as this book went to the printer, things changed: some shows moved location, others were cancelled, others increased in size or scope, others gained a focus on a particular type of item. Some flea markets may move because of urban renewal or other reasons.

Won't you please let us know? If you do, we'll be able to improve the next edition of this book. Then, future readers can benefit from your findings.

Either tear out this page, or feel free to use other sheets of paper.

Sincerely,

Peter Manston

What did you find different?

What problems did you find?

Is there any way to avoid this problem?

What markets or fairs moved time or place?

What was your greatest success and most wonderful find?

Thank you very much!

Please send your comments to:

Peter Manston
c/o B.T. Batsford
4 Fitzhardinge Street
London W1H 0AH